OSPREY AIRCRAFT OF THE ACES® • 50

# Hungarian Aces of World War 2

SERIES EDITOR: TONY HOLMES

**OSPREY AIRCRAFT OF THE ACES® • 50**

# Hungarian Aces of World War 2

György Punka

OSPREY
PUBLISHING

**Front cover**
On the morning of 9 October 1944 two fighters of 102/2 'Ricsi' Fighter Squadron took off from their base at Munkács, in Hungary, and headed for Soviet supply routes supporting the tank battle in the Debrecen area. Control of this particular sector of the frontline had been entrusted by the Luftwaffe to this unit, which was opposed by a numerically superior Soviet force.

The patrolling Messerschmitt fighters were flown by Capt László Pottyondy (in Bf 109G-6 'Blue 4') and 1/Lt Ferenc Málnássy. Flying over the eastern Carpathian Mountains, near the town of Tucholka, the Hungarian pilots spotted a large formation of Il-2s, escorted by 12 Lavochkin La-5 fighters. Passing over the main road from Stryj to Munkács, the Soviet *Stormoviks* were cruising at a height of 2000 m, with their fighter escorts 1000 m above them.

The Hungarian pilots climbed to a height of 4000 m before diving at the last two La-5s in the escort formation. Pottyondy registered 13 mm machine gun hits on his opponent from the tail up to the engine, although he failed to strike the target with his deadly 20 mm cannon. Launching a second attack, Pottyondy's rounds soon started a fire, and the La-5 began to trail smoke before abruptly banking away and spiralling down into a hill. The future 13-victory ace had just claimed his third kill.

In the meantime Málnássy had also succeeded in downing a La-5, the Soviet aeroplane 'turning inside out' before the the pilot took to his parachute – the future 11-kill ace had claimed his first victory. By this time the Il-2s had jettisoned their bombs, anxious to escape the attention of the marauding *Gustavs*. Both Hungarian pilots safely returned to base
(*Cover artwork by Iain Wyllie*)

**Back cover**
Aces three. Ranking Hungarian ace Ens Dezső Szentgyörgyi (left), Lt József Málik and Sgt Lajos Krascsenics pose for the camera in early 1945 (*Zsák via Sinka*)

First published in Great Britain in 2002 by Osprey Publishing
Elms Court, Chapel Way, Botley, Oxford, OX2 9LP

© 2002 Osprey Publishing Limited

ISBN 1 84176 436 1

Edited by Tony Holmes and Neil Maxwell
Page design by Mark Holt
Cover Artwork by Iain Wyllie
Aircraft Profiles by John Weal
Scale Drawings by Mark Styling
Origination by Grasmere Digital Imaging, Leeds, UK
Printed in China through Bookbuilders

EDITOR'S NOTE
To make this best-selling series as authoritative as possible, the Editor would be interested in hearing from any individual who may have relevant photographs, documentation or first-hand experiences relating to the world's elite pilots, and their aircraft, of the various theatres of war. Any material used will be credited to its original source. Please write to Tony Holmes at 10 Prospect Road, Sevenoaks, Kent, TN13 3UA, Great Britain, or by e-mail at:
tony.holmes@osprey-jets.freeserve.co.uk

For a catalogue of all Osprey Publishing titles please contact us at:

**Osprey Direct UK, PO Box 140, Wellingborough, Northants NN8 2FA, UK**
E-mail: **info@ospreydirect.co.uk**

**Osprey Direct USA, c/o MBI Publishing, 729 Prospect Ave, PO Box 1, Osceola, WI 54020, USA**
E-mail: **info@ospreydirectusa.com**

# CONTENTS

# THE EASTERN FRONT

On 28 June 1942 the Germans launched their great summer offensive against Stalin's forces in the Kursk region, the battle being simultaneously fought on a frontline some several hundred kilometres long. Fighting alongside the Wehrmacht and the Luftwaffe were 200,000 soldiers of the 2nd Hungarian Army and 5500 men and 90 aircraft of the 1st Air Division. The pride of the Hungarian armed forces were once again tackling the Soviet armies head on, just as they had done one year earlier during the opening phase of Operation *Barbarossa*.

The transportation of the 2nd Hungarian Army to the theatre of operations started on 17 April and was completed by 27 July. The Germans tried to surround the Soviet forces by placing themselves on the wings of the 2nd Hungarian Army as it advanced towards the River Don.

The Red Army had withdrawn some of its troops and most of its weapons from the direction of the advance well beforehand, so the first Hungarian forces pressed on quickly towards the Don, reaching it on 6 July. The Hungarians were given air support by the 1st Air Division, which from 15 October was called the 2nd Air Brigade.

The fighter coverage for Hungarian air operations during the offensive was provided by 1/1 Fighter Squadron (FS), equipped with Italian-built

A white-crossed Hungarian *Héja* sits forlornly on its belly after crash-landing on the Eastern Front in the autumn of 1942. Note the 1/1 FS badge positioned mid fuselage. The Hungarians acquired 70 Re.2000s from the Italians in 1939-40, 50 of which subsequently saw action against the Soviets in 1941-42. Obsolescent when Operation *Barbarossa* was launched in June 1941, the Reggiane fighters fought in ever dwindling numbers with the Hungarian 2nd Air Brigade until finally replaced by Bf 109F-4/Bs in mid January 1943 *(Mujzer)*

Graphically illustrating the primitive conditions confronting groundcrews during the winter of 1942-43, an Re.2000 has its Piaggio P.XI engine changed at Ilovskoje. The Reggiane's radial powerplant proved to be a mechanical nightmare 'in-the-field' (Terray via Punka)

Heir to the Hungarian throne, 1/Lt István Horthy (left) and future ace Lt Imre Pánczél relax between missions at Ilovskoje in early August 1942. Horthy's solitary combat success came on 3 August whilst leading an escort mission for a He 46 short-range reconnaissance aircraft over the river Don. He shot up a LaGG-3 which disappeared into cloud trailing smoke, and as no one saw the Soviet aircraft crash, Horthy's claim for a kill could not be confirmed (Punka Archiv)

Reggiane Re.2000s. The unit, and its 11 aircraft, arrived at the front on 1 July 1942, and by the next day had set up its base at an airfield near Kursk. 1/1 FS was following in the footsteps of 1/3 Fighter Company, which had fought on the Eastern Front from June through to December 1941, before returning home. Equipped with Fiat CR.42 biplane fighters, the company had flown 800 hours during the course of 447 missions. Its pilots had scored 17 kills (19 according to some sources) for the loss of three men (two killed and one captured) and three aircraft.

Come the summer of 1942, the Hungarians' principal fighter was the antiquated Re.2000 *Héja*, seven of which had been sent to the front on an experimental basis in the autumn of 1941. Flying alongside the CR.42s, the Reggiane pilots claimed eight kills during three months of missions for the loss of one pilot in combat and another during a ferry flight.

Within a few weeks of *Barbarossa* commencing, the Hungarian fighter pilots discovered that the enemy had the upper hand in both firepower and speed with their various Polikarpov, LaGG and MiG fighters. They also realised, however, that they could get results against their Soviet opponents if they managed to force them into a dogfight.

Returning to July 1942, 1/1 FS reached its operational destination of Ilovskoje airfield on the 13th of the month as Axis troops continued to push forward. By 3 August 11 Re.2000s of 2/1 FS had also arrived at the front, and it was intended that 1/1 FS would support bombing missions while 2/1 FS would cover short-range reconnaissance patrols.

On the 3rd five Reggianes escorted three Hungarian Caproni Ca.135 bombers sent to attack a road junction between Sredne and Ikoretz. The following day the fighters were busy from early morning to late afternoon patrolling above the bridges over the Don. The first two Re.2000s had sortied at 0415 hrs to escort a Heinkel He 46 reconnaissance aircraft, and during the course of the mission they engaged LaGG-3 fighters. 1/1 FS leader 1/Lt István Horthy succeeded in hitting a LaGG during the brief action which ensued, and the Soviet fighter disappeared into cloud trailing smoke. No one saw it crash, so the kill was disputed. The Re.2000s that took off at 0950 hrs also got into a fight, and Ens Vajda shot down two enemy aircraft.

On 7 August the fighter pilots were told to cover the 1st Armoured

1/Lt István Horthy (extreme left), and future aces Lt Imre Pánczél (third from the left) and Sgt Dezső Szentgyörgyi (sixth from left) conduct a pre-mission brief with other 1/1 FS pilots in late July 1942. Horthy was killed just weeks later when his fighter stalled and crashed soon after taking off from Ilovskoje on the morning of 18 August *(Punka Archiv)*

Division as it pushed forward, and the 1st Fighter Battalion duly reported that one of its aircraft had disappeared after an engagement with II-2s.

Although having been in action for just a few days, the Hungarians were already finding that their Re.2000s were suffering serious mechanical problems, and pilots were told to operate only in pairs.

At 1500 hrs on the 7th the Hungarian group commander reported that a pair of Reggianes flown by Maj Kálmán Csukás and Sgt Dezső Szentgyörgyi had scattered a formation of 'enemy' bombers. However, it soon emerged that their victims had in fact been three German He 111s bombing in front of the 7th Light Division. Maj Csukás claimed a bomber shot down, and the badly damaged He 111 belly-landing near the village of Korotojak. Two of the crew were injured, and the major had to apologise.

The following day 1/1 FS could put up only three fighters due to more mechanical maladies. Taking off at 0645 hrs, the trio of Re.2000s was soon reduced to just a pair when one of the pilots had to return to base with more technical faults. The remaining Reggianes attacked enemy fighters escorting a formation of bombers, although no claims were made.

That same morning two aircraft from 2/1 FS were assigned to protect troops against a possible air raid in support of an attempted enemy crossing at Alexandrovka. At 0805 hrs they intercepted 12 II-2s and a similar number of escorting fighters, although their attacks had little effect on the Soviet aircraft when the machine guns jammed on both Re.2000s. With no effective fighter force, the commander of the 1st Air Division had to ask German fighter units for help in protecting Hungarian ground forces.

Around the clock maintenance resulted in six Re.2000s being sortied between 0410 and 0530 hrs on 9 August, the fighters being sent to patrol a sector of the frontline near the village of Davidovka. At 0428 hrs 16 II-2s and a similar number of LaGG-3s flew into the area, but their progress was not checked as the first two intercepting pilots mistook the raiders for German fighters and flew on! The remaining four Hungarian pilots realised they were enemy aircraft, however, and engaged them. Lt Kázár downed a fighter attacking Lt László Molnár, and then dived close to the ground to escape from a second LaGG which was chasing him. He pulled back on the throttle and the Soviet aircraft flew past him. The Hungarian quickly took aim and fired, and his victim fell to the ground on fire. Two other LaGG-3s were downed by Capt Keresztes and Sgt Tarnay. Lt Takács was the only Hungarian casualty, being forced to crash-land behind his own lines when he was shot in the thigh and shoulder.

At 1130 hrs more patrolling fighters spotted Soviet tanks crossing the Don, and the German High Command immediately responded by ordering an attack by Junkers Ju 87 dive-bombers, which the Hungarian fighters were assigned to cover.

On the morning of 11 August an Re.2000 that was escorting an He 46 was hit by flak and brought down in enemy territory. Its pilot, Cpl Gémes, took to his parachute, but the wind carried him across to the eastern bank of the Don and he was captured.

Hungarian pilots are briefed before combat. Standing on the left is future 30.5-kill ranking Hungarian ace, Sgt Dezső Szentgyörgyi *(Punka Archiv)*

Later that same day a four-aircraft formation provided aerial support for an armoured division, as well as escorting bombers heading for targets in Korotojak and Storozhevoje. At 1230 hrs 12 LaGG-3s attempted to attack the Axis formation, but the commander of the Hungarian fighters, future 5.5-kill ace 1/Lt Pál Irányi, chased the Russians off into the clouds. When he emerged into a clear patch of sky, Irányi was surprised to find himself surrounded by five enemy fighters. Despite having been 'bounced', the Hungarian reacted faster to the threat and succeeded in shooting down one of the LaGGs – the aircraft dived away, leaving a trail of thick black smoke in its wake. At this point Irányi wisely decided to flee into nearby cloud cover, as the remaining Russian pilots were lining up an attack. Irányi duly returned home.

Air patrols and bomber escort missions continued unabated, and further aerial combat took place on the 17th when an He 46 was set upon by a Russian fighter. The escorting pair of Re.2000s quickly intervened and the communist pilot broke off his attack.

Shortly after 0500 hrs on 18 August two fighters led by 1/Lt István Horthy (flying his 25th operational sortie), the Hungarian Deputy Regent, set out as escorts for a reconnaissance aircraft. Horthy's Re.2000 (V.421) stalled and crashed as it attempted to climb away from the airfield, killing the heir to the Hungarian throne. Later that same day Sgt István Baltai disappeared during an engagement, and the wreckage of his aircraft was found weeks later by advancing Axis troops.

At 0500 hrs on 2 September 1/Lt Irányi led 1/1 FS on a patrol over the villages of Korotojak and Svoboda. The unit soon came across four Il-2s, which the Hungarians attacked from above in order to shoot out the vulnerable radiator mounted above the *Stormovik's* engine. Irányi's victim crashed, and his wingman, Sgt Zoltán Raposa, also scored hits on a second Il-2, although it was not seen to hit the ground. They were covered by Lt Orssich and Cadet Lajos Molnár during the attack.

Russian flak units got involved at this point, paying little heed to the fact that they might shoot down their own aircraft. Cadet Molnár's machine was hit, with the 20 mm round ripping off two of his fingers. Yet despite his painful wounds, he managed to belly-land just 500 m from the

1/1 FS's Lt Imre Pánczél poses in his 'Dongó' (wasp) marked Re. 2000 *Héja*. The first Hungarian ace of World War 2, Pánczél scored seven kills (all Il-2s) in the final three months of 1942, three of which were downed on consecutive days flying an Re.2000 of 2/1 FS *(Pagáts via Punka)*

Don, luckily in friendly territory. His Re.2000 was the last of four lost in August-September, and a further six fighters were damaged.

In October the pilots of 1/1 FS were removed from the frontline to commence conversion onto the Bf 109, leaving 2/1 FS to operate the surviving Re.2000s from Ilovskoje. That same month future 7-kill ace Lt Imre Pánczél and Ens László Kovács-Nagy, both formerly with 1/1 FS, were transferred to 2/1 FS. Lt Pánczél achieved his first victory on the 29th, his second on the 30th and his third on the 31st, all while flying with Ens Kovács-Nagy. All three kills were over Il-2s, with his final victory coming during a fight with 22 *Stormoviks*. Ens Kovács-Nagy was also credited with a kill on the 31st, while a third Il-2 fell to an unknown pilot.

In early November a further four pilots left Ilovskoje to commence the Bf 109 conversion course, and from then until the first week of December, the Re.2000s rarely flew. On 25 November 5/2 FS arrived at the front, led by Capt Gyula Horváth, and it took over the remaining *Héjas* in order to complete the training it had started in Hungary.

During December Soviet forces broke through the Italian 8th Army's frontline to the right of the Hungarian 2nd Army. New communist air-fields were set up, and enemy rail traffic also increased. The nature of Soviet troop movements just behind the frontline made it almost impossible for Axis forces to work out when the communist forces planned to attack next, and it fell to the Hungarian 2nd Air Brigade to mount reconnaissance and bombing missions to disrupt enemy preparations for an assault. However, the brigade could not carry out its role effectively partly because of bad weather, and also because of a total lack of bombers.

By the time the Red Army launched its offensive on 12 January 1943, Hungarian Air Force units were operating successfully in spite of the weather, although they were unable to exert much influence on events.

The last air combat in the area was fought at 1230 hrs on the opening day of the assault by 1/Lt József Bejczy (in Re.2000 V.440) and his wingman Sgt Pál Domján (in V.439). Their job was to escort German bombers as part of a free-fighting operation between Storoshevoje-Staraja and Kevroston-Yariv. However, upon spotting their Hungarian escorts, the Ju 87s, Ju 88s, He 111s and Hs 126s fled into a thick layer of cloud, having mistaken the Re.2000s for Russian fighters! Minutes later a twin-engined Soviet fighter attacked the leading *Héja* through a hole in the clouds, but Bejczy turned into the aggressor and it fled eastwards.

On 14 and 15 January the Re.2000s performed uneventful patrol and reconnaissance missions. These would be the war-weary Reggianes final flights, as with no time to heat the fighters' frozen engine oil, and with Soviet forces rapidly approaching Ilovskoje, Hungarian groundcrews blew up the last unserviceable *Héjas* between 16 and 19 January.

# THE FIRST HUNGARIAN Bf 109s

In October 1942 the Luftwaffe agreed to re-equip part of the Hungarian fighter force with the Bf 109. At this time the Hungarian Air Force High Command decided to replace 1 Fighter Group Command and 2/1 FS with 5/I Fighter Group and 5/2 FS. These designation changes would come into effect on 15 December. Up until then 5/I Fighter Group (FG) had been responsible for the defence of Budapest.

In November Capt Aladár Heppes, the unit's commander (and a future 8-kill ace), went to the front to assess the situation regarding the relocation of 5/2 FS, then commanded by Capt Horváth. The 5/2 FS pilots, meanwhile, continued their conversion training in an active military area, as did the eight pilots of 1/1 FS, led by 1/Lt György Bánlaky, who had been attached to the Bf 109-equipped JG 52 at Stary Oskol.

Once the retraining of 1/1 FS had been completed, the Germans supplied the unit with six used Bf 109F-4/Bs and the Hungarians were absorbed within a *staffel* (led by Gefreiter Verb Neubert) of I./JG 52. The unit was flying fighter-bomber missions from Urasovo at the time, helping to prop up the Italian front, which had been broken by the Soviets. Their targets were tanks hiding in the forests, as well as trucks and trains.

On 25 October the Hungarian pilots completed their first combat sorties in the Bf 109, and by November regular fighter-bomber missions were being flown. The 1 *'Ungarische' Jabostaffel* (Hungarian Fighter-Bomber Squadron) was born.

Mid-way through the month the weather changed on the front, and strong winds and heavy snow made flying impossible. However, a mission

Mechanics prepare an ETC 50/VII rack and 250 kg bombs prior to this Bf 109F-4/B being sent out on its next mission in late 1942. Many of the Hungarian pilots who flew the F-model Messerschmitt on fighter-bomber operations found it easier to handle than their colleagues who used it solely as an interceptor *(Petrick)*

Partially marked in Hungarian colours (note the white stripe over the swastika on the fighter's tail), this aircraft is manhandled into position alongside Bf 109F-4/B 'Yellow 7' at Poltava in late February 1943 (*archiv Kiss*)

Ens Tivadar Gyenis runs up the engine of Bf 109F-4/B V-+08 on the snow-covered airfield at Rossosh in December 1942. In the weeks prior to this photograph being taken, the Axis powers were occupying the largest area of the Soviet Union that they would hold during the entire war (*Fekets via Punka*)

was flown by the '*Ungarische' Jabostaffel* on the 29th, in company with other pilots from I./JG 52 and Italian fighter units. The Axis aircraft searched the forests between Buturlinovka and Koslovka for hidden Soviet tanks.

16 December was a landmark day for the Hungarian unit, as its commander, Lt Imre Pánczél, downed four Il-2s (two in the morning and two in the afternoon) to raise his score to seven. Not only was he the first Hungarian to claim victories with the Bf 109, he had also become the first Hungarian ace of World War 2. By the end of 1942 1/1 FS had completed 140 sorties with the Bf 109 (mostly fighter-bomber missions), and during this period it had not lost a single aircraft over enemy territory.

Part of 5/1 FS arrived at the front on 26 December, commanded by future 7-kill ace Capt György Újszászy. The pilots of 1/1 FS showed no interest in flying under the leadership of a new squadron commander, however, so Újszászy and his men commenced training flights at Stary Oskol on their own! In the meantime, Capt Heppes, with 5/2 FS, and the 5/I FG Staff had also started their conversion onto the Bf 109.

A real Russian winter arrived with January 1943. The sky was overcast, with a cloud base of just 100 m, and heavy falls of snow were blown by strong winds into large drifts across the Axis airfields. Nevertheless, the low-level attacks had to be continued at full strength, and at all costs, because reconnaissance reports revealed significant movement of Soviet forces behind the frontline. Due to the low cloud, the Bf 109 pilots had to release their bombs at a very low altitude. This made aiming more difficult and flak more effective. There was also the Soviet Air Force to contend with, and against large numbers of enemy aircraft I./JG 52 and the small Hungarian group barely presented an effective opposition. Meanwhile, in the skies over Kantemirovka, American-made Tomahawk fighters and Boston bombers made their first appearance.

11 January was a black day for the Hungarians. Lt Pánczél and Ens István Szabó took off for a fighter sortie at 1130 hrs, having been briefed

to fly over Svoboda, Davidovka and Korotoiak. Neither pilot returned. In the evening the news arrived that a Bf 109 had gone down and been burnt out between Ostrogoshk and Kopanche. Identification documents that survived the fire revealed Lt Pánczél to have been the pilot.

As previously mentioned, Imre Pánczél had been Hungary's first ace. In October 1942 he had successfully fought three air engagements as the leader of four *Héja* aircraft, with one of these actions occurring when a mixed force of 12 Soviet fighters and bombers attacked the railway line between Podgarnoje and Kamenka. Although outnumbered, the four Hungarian pilots claimed five victories in 22 minutes. Three of the five enemy aircraft were shot down by Pánczél, although his third victory was not confirmed – this aircraft was hit several times and crash-landed in front of the Hungarian lines, where it was blasted apart by artillery fire.

Between 6 and 10 December, having converted onto the Bf 109, Pánczél knocked out three locomotives, 17 vehicles and a flak battery with his bombs. His four aerial victories on 12 December raised his total to seven. Pánczél was the leading scorer in the Hungarian Air Force at the time of his death, and Hungarian Regent Adm Miklós Horthy posthumously awarded him the Knight's Cross of the Hungarian Order with ribbons and swords.

On the morning of 13 January 1943 the communist guns on the Eastern Front began to roar. Within hours, Soviet armoured forces had broken through the weak defences of the 2nd Hungarian Army in several

**V-+08's frontline career did not last overly long, for it was written off in this crash-landing at Rossosh in January 1943. Note that its tail section has been partially severed *(Fekets via Punka)***

**Also seen at Rossosh, these winter-camouflaged Bf 109Fs carry a mixture of German and Hungarian markings. Groundcrews had little chance to repaint whole aircraft due to the number of missions that were being flown at the time. Indeed, in many cases only the national colours (red-white-green) applied to the fighters' fin and rudder distinguished partly-repainted Hungarian Bf 109s from German ones. Taking off behind the Messerschmitts are three Ju 87s, and parked behind the fighters are two He 111s *(Kovács via Punka)***

places and penetrated deep into Axis territory. The defence of the River Don ordered by Hitler became hopeless.

On 14 January 5/I FG headquarters had been ordered to set up a ring of ground defences around Urasovo airfield. Under the command of Lt Col Kálmán Csukás (a member of the General Staff), some 750 armed air and groundcrew and a few 40 mm Bofors flak guns represented the entire defensive force. They had no mortars or anti-tank guns, and the bulk of their heavy weaponry consisted of cannon and machine guns hastily stripped out of grounded aircraft.

Bf 109G-1 V-+5 is seen in this rather strangely posed picture taken on an airfield in Russia in early 1943. Due to a chronic shortage of aircraft, all Hungarian Bf 109s were usually shared amongst the pilots. Parked behind the *Gustav* is an Me 321 *Gigant* glider transport *(Sinka via Punka)*

Due to the increasing number of attacks by partisans, and the approach of Soviet tanks, serviceable aircraft were flown out while the unserviceable ones were blown up. On 17 January several thousand escaping and unarmed Hungarian, German and Italian soldiers reached the airfield. Around 800 of them were wounded and frost-bitten. That same day the Red Army surrounded Urasovo, and within 24 hours permission came through to break out. After the arrival of the rear guard of the German 26th 'Westfalen' Infantry Division, they broke out to the west on the 20th, reaching Novy-Oskol on 23 January.

Two days later Capt Heppes took command of 5/I FG, now based in Kiev, along with 5/2 FS, a maintenance squadron and the remnants of the 5/1 FS. In the meantime, Bánlaky's flight within I./JG 52 continued to see action. At dawn on 15 January, Russian tanks attacked the group's airfield at Rossosh, and three serviceable aircraft were evacuated to Ilovskoje. Aircraft from JG 52, along with Ju 87s, started to strafe and bomb their own recently-abandoned airfield, knocking out a number of tanks. However, they could not hold back the second attack, and in the afternoon the unflyable German aircraft at Rossosh were blown up. Evacuation took place to Kharkov on 18 January, and later to Kursk.

Several days later the Germans handed over Kursk-East airfield to the Hungarians, and on the 28th two aircraft arrived at the new site. However, they did not stay long, returning to Kharkov-East on 4 February. On the 9th the Hungarians evacuated four aircraft to Poltava, while a fifth had to be blown up. On the 16th they received new Messerschmitts, and the older

These variously marked Hungarian Bf 109Fs have been parked into wind at Rossosh airfield in December 1942, ready to scramble at a moment's notice. Note that they have had their landing gear doors removed. Within a month of this photograph being taken, Red Army armoured units had broken through the weak defences of the 2nd Hungarian Army, and at dawn on 15 January tanks attacked Rossosh airfield. By then only three serviceable Hungarian Bf 109s remained at the base, and these were hastily evacuated to Ilovskoje *(Jávor)*

1/1 FS's Lt László Kovács-Nagy, Ens Ottó Lukács, 1/Lt György Bánlaky and Sgt Dezső Szentgyörgyi converse soon after being awarded the Iron Cross, First Class, in the early spring of 1943. Other recipients of this medal were Sgt/Maj István Fábián (one of the first Hungarian pilots to receive it) and Cpl/Maj Ernö Kiss, who on 16 March 1945 would score the last 'Puma' victory of World War 2 *(Punka Archiv)*

Enduring harsh winter conditions in early 1943, Sgt Dezső Szentgyörgyi (right) and his mechanic pose alongside their Bf 109F-4/B V-+07 at Rossosh. Note the crudely-applied white winter camouflage, which has suffered heavy weathering from the cockpit forward *(Punka Archiv)*

Bf 109F-4 V-+25 basks in the welcome spring sunshine at Umany airfield in 1943. Parked in the distance are *Jagdwaffe* Bf 109Gs and Fw 190As. As German forces mounted counter-attacks on the Soviet advances north of the base, the Hungarian fighters were almost always in the air either protecting Axis bombers or carrying out patrols *(Frank via Petrick)*

machines were handed over to 5/I FG – the group had recommenced training on the Bf 109 on 20 January at Umany airfield following a hasty evacuation further westward. This time the conversion was better organised, being run by a larger staff of instructors so as to achieve combat readiness in the shortest time possible.

Meanwhile, '*Ungarische*' *Jabostaffel* continued to fly combat missions, and on 20, 21 and 22 February its pilots carried out low-level strafing and bombing attacks against trucks, cavalry and sleighs.

This routine of fighter-bomber missions dragged on into March, with Bánlaky's men flying missions from Poltava in support of the German counter-attack to recapture Kharkov. At the end of the month the unit moved to the recaptured Kharkov-South airfield at Osnava. On 13 April the battle-weary 1/Lt György Bánlaky was recalled to Hungary, having led his unit in action for nine solid months.

By then, 5/I FG Staff had also switched bases to Kharkov, where it had been combined with 5/1 FS.

The snow at Rossosh claims another victim. Groundcrew attach ropes to the tail section of V-+03 and prepare to bring it back to earth. Only minimal damage was inflicted on the precious fighter *(Punka Archiv)*

Ens Ottó Lukács enjoys a cigarette whilst huddled alongside his bombed-up Bf 109F-4/B at Ilovskoje. Lukács was awarded the Iron Cross, First Class, for his early combat record flying the Messerschmitt fighter-bomber *(Terray via Punka)*

Now fully trained on the Bf 109, the Hungarian pilots started to fly fighter-bomber missions in conjunction with I./JG 51, which was commanded by Hauptmann Hans-Günther von Fassong.

With 5/I FG now committed to action, Aladár Heppes was promoted to the rank of major, and the group commander flew his first mission on 6 April. 5/1 FS's squadron commander flew his first mission 20 days later.

On the 27th Capt György Újszászy shot down his first Il-2, followed by an La-5 the following day. However, because there had been no witnesses to these victories, 5/I FG was not officially credited with its first kill until the morning of 29 April when, at 0700 hrs, six Soviet Bostons, escorted by a large number of fighters, attacked Kharkov-Osnava airfield. A flight of four Hungarian aircraft had been made ready to defend the base from just such an attack, and they duly scrambled. The first flight, led by Lt József Bejczy of 5/I FG Staff, consisted of Sgt Tarnay, future

Lt György Debrődy (second left) meets pilots from I./JG 51, including *Gruppenkommandeur* Hauptmann Hans-Günther von Fassong (third from left), in April 1943. Pilots of 5/1 FS were flying fighter-bomber missions with the German unit from Kharkov at the time. Debrődy ended the war with 20 victories *(Winkler Archiv)*

14.5-kill ace Cpl István Fábián (who was nicknamed 'Koponya' ('Skull') because of his large head) and Sgt Károly Kereki of 5/1 FS. Bejczy hit an engine of one of the Bostons before his cannon jammed and the bomber, although smoking, got away. Tarnay enjoyed better luck, chasing another Soviet bomber and shooting it down for his second confirmed victory – his first had come while flying a *Héja* in 1942.

From 6 May 1943 onwards, six air armies of the Soviet Air Force (the 1st Western Front, 15th Briansk Front, 16th Central Front, 2nd Voronezh Front, 17th South-West Front and 18th South Front) attacked numerous Axis airfields in order to destroy aircraft on the ground. Seventeen bases were hit in the first strikes on the 6th, although the Luftwaffe was quick to get airborne and the Soviets failed in their objective.

However, the May air offensive is considered to be the greatest and most important operation of the Soviets' Great Patriotic War. Communist aircraft flew 1400 sorties in just 72 hours, destroying 500 aircraft and losing 122 of their own. Still, they could not defeat German air power, which continued to attack railway junctions, factories and airfields.

With the arrival of 5/2 FS in the frontline just as the offensive commenced, Hungarian fighter-bomber missions ceased for the time being. The newly-arrived squadron, called the *'Frontjäger'* (frontline fighter) by the Germans, was given new Bf 109F-4s optimised for fighter interception – during the course of May the unit received 19 new aircraft.

5/2 FS flew both defensive patrols and escorted bombers in its first weeks in combat. During one of these escort missions, on the 30th, six Bf 109s, commanded by Maj Heppes, flew from Kharkov to protect German bombers heading for Valuiki. As the formation neared its target, 12 Soviet fighters scrambled from nearby Kupinsk airfield and attacked. Maj Heppes and his wingman, Lt Lipták, broke off to meet the enemy. While four escorts remained with the bombers, the two Hungarian pilots became embroiled in a dogfight, eventually shooting down two Yak-1s.

To get an idea of the relative power balance between the combatants, accounts highlight the events of 2 June, when Luftwaffe aircraft in five waves (424 bombers and 119 fighters) attacked the Kursk railway junction. The Soviet Air Force sent up 106 fighters to oppose them.

Maj Aladár Heppes was commander of 5/I FG. Finishing the war with eight kills, he saw extensive service on the Eastern Front, and as the tide of war threatened Hungary itself, the 'Old Puma', by then aged 40, was put in charge of 101 Home Defence Fighter Group *(Punka Archiv)*

Capt György Újszászy, commander of 5/I FS, leaps out of the cockpit after claiming another kill. He 'made ace' when he downed two Il-2s on 13 July 1943 *(Kovács via Punka)*

Hot summer work for the groundcrew as they prepare to arm this Bf 109F-4/B for a fighter-bomber mission from Kharkov. 5/I FG's 'Puma' marking is clearly visible on the nose of the Messerschmitt. The remaining three Hungarian aircraft parked in the middle distance are also being bombed up *(Papp via Punka)*

Even the best pilots could come unstuck. This newly-delivered Bf 109F-4/B (radio code SF+JP), seen being retrieved by an Italian Ansaldo light tank, was being flown by Lt György Debrődy on 25 April 1943 when he was forced to belly-land with engine trouble. Debrődy would score 18 victories on the Eastern Front and a further 6.5 kills in the defence of Hungary (Terray via Punka)

Serving as a backdrop for two unidentified groundcrewmen, V.0+39 was the Bf 109F-4/B flown by Maj Aladár Heppes during 5/I FG's spell at Kharkov in 1943. Heppes claimed his first victory (a Yak-1) in this aircraft on 30 May near Kupiansk (Punka Archiv)

The first wave consisted of 130 bombers and 30 escort fighters, and the Russians shot down 58 of them. The second and third waves were made up of 120 bombers and 55 fighters, and the Germans lost 34 shot down by 86 Soviet fighters. The fourth and fifth waves consisted of 167 bombers and just 14 fighters, and they were intercepted by the Russians over Kursk at between 6000 m and 7000 m.

From these waves about 100 aircraft broke through the Soviet fighter defence and destroyed the railway junction. According to communist estimates, the Germans lost a total of 145 aircraft. This was the last mass daytime attack by the Luftwaffe during the Great Patriotic War. During this period the Hungarian fighters were deployed mainly on escort duties.

At 0400 hrs on 26 June Sgt Dezső Szentgyörgyi, accompanied by Cpl-Maj István Fábián, departed on a yet another escort mission. This was Szentgyörgyi's 92nd operational sortie since his arrival in the USSR in mid 1942, and in that time he had achieved only one 'victory' – a German He 111 bomber! This unfortunate case of misidentification had occurred when the Heinkel was spotted bombing newly-captured Hungarian positions on a seesawing frontline.

Returning to 26 June 1943, the Hungarians were escorting bombers sent to attack Grasnoie airfield. The intercepting Soviet fighters outnumbered the 1/1 FS Bf 109s five-to-one, but the Hungarians took up the challenge. Szentgyörgyi downed a Yak-1 and Fábián saw off a second.

By July 1943 Soviet air power had nearly doubled since April, with the number of communist aircraft available rising by between 750 and 800 once reserves were received from High Command. On the main sectors at the front, air division strength totalled 1200 aircraft.

## THE BATTLE OF KURSK

The struggle for air superiority was at its fiercest during the spring and summer of 1943, reaching its peak during the German offensive at Kursk. At the beginning of July, the

An impromptu briefing is conducted alongside unusually spotless Bf 109F-4/B 'Yellow 7' in early 1943. The pilot standing at the extreme right is Sgt Szentgyörgi (*archiv Kiss*)

In his element, Sgt Szentgyörgi pulls up alongside his camera-toting wingman in Bf 109F-4/B 'Red 2', which boasts Luftwaffe crosses and Hungarian red, white and green tail markings (*archiv Kiss*)

Germans, trying to turn the tide, started a wide-scale push towards Kursk. The Wehrmacht was supported in its campaign by both *Luftflotten* 4 and 6, who had almost 1000 aircraft concentrated on airfields in the Oriol salient. A similar number were gathered near Kharkov and Poltava, half of which were bombers.

Against them were pitted the air divisions of the Soviet 16th Central Front, 2nd Voronezh Front and the 17th South-West Front, together with a long-range bomber division and the 5th Air Division of the Steppe Area Air Command.

According to post-war Soviet researchers, the number of aircraft immediately available – 2072 – was nearly the same as the German total. However, this figure does not include the 3000 aircraft in the overall command area of the South-West Front, and a further 880 in the Steppe Area Command. The latter were assigned to other sectors along the front, although they could have been transferred to the Kursk area if needed.

Unlike previous campaigns, the Germans would not enjoy the element of surprise at Kursk, for Soviet aerial reconnaissance units had spotted Wehrmacht troop and tank concentrations prior to the launching of the ground offensive. This meant that the Soviet High Command was not only prepared for the attack, but actually started a counter-attack.

At dawn on 5 July Soviet bomber formations attacked eight Axis airfields. Although it became obvious to the Germans that their plans had been discovered, it was too late to stop their war machinery, and at

0530 hrs Operation *Citadel* commenced along a 40 km-wide front.

During the day 2300 German aircraft were seen in the central sector of the front alone. At times 300 Axis bombers and at least 100 fighters were counted over the battlefield at once. Dogfights were constant, involving hundreds of aircraft from both sides. However, significant tactical errors were made by the Soviet fighter pilots, for in the heat of battle they often forgot about the German bombers, allowing them to break through and reach their original targets. Soviet ground forces were devastated.

The Hungarian fighter force, now dubbed the 'Pumas' and stationed at Varvasovka airfield, was alerted at 0300 hrs on 5 July when observers reported the approach of Soviet bombers. 5/1 FS was held back to defend the airfield while 5/2 FS engaged the attackers.

Future aces 1/Lts Miklós Kenyeres and István Kálmán were the first pilots scrambled at 0330 hrs, and they were immediately set upon by La-5s. Fending off the fighters, the pilots attacked a formation of Il-2s, and after firing at a *Stormovik* at close range near the rear of the formation, Kenyeres broke away, giving Kálmán the chance to claim his first kill.

The Soviet fighters then returned, forcing the Hungarians to flee, and it was then that Kenyeres lost sight of his wingman. He then spotted another 1/1 FS pilot flying without a wingman, and this turned out to be future 5.5-kill ace Sgt Pál Kovács. Kenyeres tipped his wings, indicating to Kovács to take up the wingman position, and soon they joined up with three German fighters patrolling nearby. Shortly afterwards they attacked eight Il-2s, and Kovács claimed two kills and Kenyeres one – the first victories for both aces. The following day Maj Heppes downed his third kill of the war when he destroyed an Il-2 over Volchansk, and future 6-kill ace 1/Lt József Bejczy got a Yak-1 to open his account.

On the 7th Capt György Ujszászy (who already had four kills to his credit) and Cpl/Maj Fábián were patrolling over the River Donietz when they intercepted six La-5s. Ujszászy hit one of them, although the smoking Russian aircraft managed to escape. On the same day Lt György Debrődy downed an Il-2 (his second victory) and Sgt Szentgyörgyi got an La-5. Debrődy's aircraft was hit by flak soon afterwards, and he was forced to make an emergency landing near Varvasovka.

According to wartime records, the Hungarian fighter group scored its 33rd kill on 20 July – 17 of these had been claimed during the Kursk offensive. This campaign was extremely tough on the pilots, and it was not unusual for them to fly four or five missions a day.

The Wehrmacht's offensive soon ran out of steam in the face of numerically superior enemy forces, and its divisions began retreating along the entire front. The Germans tried to slow down the thrust of the Soviet

The Axis air forces suffered heavy attrition whilst participating in the huge tanks battle of 1943. Here, yet another wrecked fighter (in this case an Fw 190A) is dumped in an aircraft graveyard at an unidentified location. In the foreground is ex-Hungarian Bf 109G-4/Trop Wk-Nr 16124 *(Terray via Punka)*

Lt György Debrődy (centre) poses with unnamed Hungarian pilots outside Kharkov railway station in 1943. Ace Debrődy's adventures were not always in the air, for after being hit by a Yak and force-landing 15 kms behind enemy lines, he avoided capture by fleeing into a forest and swimming across the ice-cold River Dnieper, arriving back at his base two days later *(Kovács via Punka)*

Bf 109F-4/B V.0+37 undergoes major repairs at an unidentified location. The detached left wing allows a good view of the Messerschmitt's less robust undercarriage *(Terray via Punka)*

armour with desperate counter-attacks such as at the bridgehead at Oriol. In order to hold this position, dedicated air support was required, and 5/I FG was one of the units given the job of helping to defend it. The Hungarians were re-equipped for the task, receiving Bf 109F-4s and G-2s – three on 7 July, two on the 10th, one on the 15th and ten the following day. Only seven of these aircraft were brand new.

The German 37th Division, which was defending this area, was protected from the air by more than 2200 aircraft. However, the Luftwaffe was opposed by close to 5000 Soviet aircraft. Axis troops caught in a pincer movement by the rapidly advancing Red Army defended themselves bravely, but their situation quickly deteriorated as losses mounted.

By 20 July the 'Pumas' had flown 700 missions, and as the newer pilots became more experienced so the tally grew to 1181 by month-end. July had seen the unit down 33 Soviet aircraft, drop 60.5 tons of bombs, destroy 153 vehicles and knock out eight guns.

On 1 August newly-crowned ace Capt György Újszászy and 1/Lt József Bejczy had just run into heavy 'friendly' German flak north of Belgorod. when the latter pilot spotted a formation of Soviet Petlyakov Pe-2 twin-engined bombers below them. He radioed Újszászy, who immediately closed up behind the Russians and opened fire on the rear bomber. Its gunner returned the fire, but apparently he was hit because his weapon suddenly fell silent. The bomber nose-dived and went into the ground. Újszászy had just claimed his seventh, and last, kill.

In the meantime Bejczy had positioned himself behind another Petlyakov. The pilot of the sleek twin-finned aircraft must have thought that he was being mistakenly attacked by one of his own, for he tipped his wings in an attempt to identify himself. The Hungarian made a second pass, and this time he opened fire. Bejczy's victory (his fourth kill) was confirmed both by Axis troops and other Hungarian pilots in the area.

On 3 August Soviet troops started a counter-attack in the direction of Belgorod-Kharkov. After an artillery barrage and bombing missions at dawn, armoured units broke through the frontline and advanced 30 kms on the first day. Two days later they liberated Belgorod. Incoming German reserves were attacked near Kharkov by the 8th Air Army, assigned to the Southern Front, and the 17th Air Army, assigned to the South-West Front, and, finally, by more than 1300 aircraft of the 5th Voronezh and 2nd Steppe Front air armies.

At dawn that same day 1/Lt Debrődy and Cpl/Maj János Mátyás engaged 30 Il-2s, escorted by Yak and Lavochkin fighters, north of Belgorod. Debrődy fired without result, but after an attack by his wingman one of the Il-2s burst into flames and crashed – this was Mátyás's fourth kill

Two groundcrewmen crank the engine starter handle on their Bf 109F-4/B (fitted with SC 50 bombs under its belly) whilst a shirtless colleague watches proceedings from the wingtip. The patchy grass and bare flesh date this photograph as the summer of 1943. These aircraft endured a heavy work-load during the spring and summer offensives of 1943, as the 'Pumas' always had more pilots than aircraft. This meant that the Bf 109s were frequently in the air, performing patrols, fighter-bombing, bomber escort and close support for soldiers in the frontline *(Bagossy via Punka)*

The battered remains of Bf 109F-4/B V.0+32 are the focus of much attention as the fighter-bomber lies wrecked in a field following a particularly violent crash-landing. Its unnamed pilot stayed with the aircraft, and he managed to extricate himself from the cockpit unscathed *(Zsák)*

to date. Debrődy made a second attack on four more Il-2s, and this time he succeeded in downing a *Stormovik* (his third kill).

At 0705 hrs on the 3rd 1/Lt Tibor Papp and Sgt Szentgyörgyi also engaged Il-2s over Belgorod, and each pilot claimed one shot down. Maj Heppes and 1/Lt Bejczy were also airborne that morning, escorting He 111s bombers. Their formation was duly attacked by Yak-1s, and Heppes shot down one of them (his fourth kill). He subsequently ran out of fuel whilst attempting to make it back to base, force-landing behind his own lines. Hours later Heppes was spotted by the crew of a German reconnaissance aircraft, which duly sent in another machine to pick him up.

Building on their early morning success, Papp and Szentgyörgyi each downed an La-5 on the afternoon of 3 August, taking the 'Pumas' kill tally for the day to seven. This success made Dezső Szentgyörgyi an ace, and the following day he destroyed yet another Il-2 and an La-5.

On 8 August new ace 1/Lt Debrődy (he had downed his fifth kill 48 hours earlier) and his wingman, future five-kill ace Ens Sándor Hautzinger, attacked 20 Yak-1s, and each claimed a kill. Two days later, during an afternoon patrol, Hautzinger claimed another kill when he downed an Il-2 that was attacking Kharkov-North airfield.

Between the 3rd and the 8th, Hungarian pilots had taken part in more than 20 missions a day, and several new aces had been created.

On 11 August the outer defensive ring around the city of Kharkov came under attack, and a day later the Germans hit back with 400 tanks. The Luftwaffe supported this armoured thrust with formations of between 20 and 50 aircraft. However, the operation became bogged down after driving just 20 kms into Soviet territory. With Kharkov now in danger of falling into communist hands, the Hungarian fighter units were evacuated to Poltava.

5/1 FS had now been continuously involved in the fighting on the Eastern Front since 26 December 1942, while the Group Staff and 5/2 FS had entered the fray on 1 June 1943. Some of the more battle-weary Hungarian pilots were duly sent on leave following the withdrawal from Kharkov, replacements arriving in Poltava in mid August. By then, the 'Pumas' had flown 1500 sorties and shot down 43 aircraft. During attacks on troop concentrations and transport columns, they had also destroyed more than 150 vehicles and flak sites.

On 26 August troops of the Soviet Central Front started to push towards Kiev, and by the end of the month they had broken through on a 100 km-wide front. Meanwhile, aircraft of the Soviet 2nd and 16th Air Armies were harassing the retreating German troops day and night, as well as bombing airfields and railway junctions.

At the end of the month an order came through to withdraw 5/I FG Staff and 5/1 FS. This was partly achieved through the reshuffling of personnel, with pilots who did not have enough hours on active service in combat being sent to 5/2 FS. This unit carried on with its daily tasks, flying fighter sorties, escorting bombers and mounting low-level attacks.

5 September proved to be a day of celebration for 5/I FG, as future 26-kill ace Lt Lajos Tóth scored his first and the 'Pumas'' 50th victory.

Three days later the Hungarian fighters were in action around Novaia-Vologda when 1/Lt Kőhalmy and his wingman Lt Molnár let a formation of Il-2s pass beneath them before attacking their Yak-1 escorts. The ensuing dogfight was vicious, Kőhalmy getting on the tail of one of the fighters and firing a burst in its direction. The Yak disappeared in a sharp turn, and it later came to light that a ground observation post had seen it crash.

Leaving the fighters, the pair attacked the Il-2s, which formed up in a tight defensive circle in an attempt to protect each other. Whilst the Hungarians tried to penetrate the circle, the surviving Russian fighters in turn got in behind the Bf 109s and positioned themselves for an attack. Realising the danger he was in, Kőhalmy escaped in a dive, then pulled up and shot down one of the ground-attack aircraft. At the same time the left wing of Kőhalmy's machine was hit, so he broke away from the fight and returned to base. His wingman also downed a Yak-1 in flames.

The Wehrmacht eventually halted the Soviet attack, but suffered huge losses in the process. With all reserves exhausted, retreat for the Axis forces was now unavoidable. Compressing the frontline partially helped the German cause, as did the Red Army's withdrawal of five tank divisions for re-equipment.

Supporting the Soviet troops of the Central Front in their attacks during this period was the 16th Air Army, whose effectiveness was reduced due to the constant relocation of its units. There also seemed to be a problem

The pathetic remains of an Il-2 are examined by unnamed Hungarian personnel after the *Stormovik* was shot down by the 'Pumas' during the Battle of Kursk. The tactic that the Hungarians employed to bring down these rugged machines was to attack them from below and aim for their engine-mounted radiator. The tail surfaces of this Il-2 also appear to have been badly shot up. Note the unexploded Soviet bomb propped up on its nose in front of the airman on the left *(Punka Archiv)*

over the air army's main role, with its squadrons trying to gain air superiority whilst simultaneously knocking out Axis airfields.

The heaviest air battles of the campaign took place during the offensive against German troops securing the roads to Kiev. Soviet bomber formations of between 100 and 160 aircraft-strong were regular committed, and fierce clashes took place over the Desna, Dnieper and Pripiat bridgeheads. According to official reports, pilots of the 2nd Air Army participated in 212 aerial engagements in September, downing 198 Axis aircraft.

# THE 'PUMAS' RETREAT

In the wake of the Axis defeat at Kursk, and the numerous battles that followed, the 'Pumas' moved base with depressing regularity. They fled firstly to Karlovka, then to Kiev, and finally, at the end of September, to Ushin. By then 5/1 FS had been withdrawn from combat, although 5/2 FS, led by Capt Gyula Horváth, remained in the frontline.

On the morning of 15 September, 1/Lt György Debrödy and Sgt Pál Kovács received an order to escort a formation of He 111s heading for Soviet positions. Flying below the overcast at a height of 4000 m, the Hungarians were waiting for the bombers to arrive at the rendezvous point when they spotted a formation of Yak-9s. By the time the Soviets realised they had company, the 5/2 FS pilots had launched their attack.

Two of the Russians fled into cloud, while the remaining pair initially dived before pulling up and turning back into the Messerschmitts. After surviving the frontal attack, Debrödy, who was now being chased by a Yak, pulled up into the cloud base in a left-hand climbing turn. His pursuer in

**Top**
Groundcrew pose alongside Maj Aladár Heppes Bf 109F-4/B V-0+39 in the late summer of 1943. Fitted with a DB 605A-1 engine, this aircraft features a 5/I FG badge on its nose *(Punka Archiv)*

**Bottom**
Hungarian crosses are painted onto the underside of a Bf 109G-2/R6's wings. More and more often the narrow red-white-green Hungarian national marking was painted only on the fighter's fin and rudder. Note the underwing cannon gondola, containing a single Mauser MG 151 20 mm weapon *(Kovács via Punka)*

turn broke off his attack, which was exactly what Debrödy was hoping he would do. Closing in behind the fleeing Yak, the Hungarian ace hit the Soviet fighter hard in the wing, engine and cockpit with machine gun and cannon rounds.

Seconds later Debrödy's *Gustav* was riddled by machine gun rounds from a second Yak, and as he tried to shake off his attacker his engine lost power and flames shot out from beneath the engine cowling. The Yak was still glued to the Hungarian's tail, firing more rounds into the now doomed Messerschmitt. Realising that he was too low to bail out, Debrödy was forced to crash land 15 kms inside Soviet territory, close to a flak battery. He wasted no time fleeing into a nearby forest.

Avoiding the enemy, and swimming across the icy River Dnieper, Debrödy made it back to base two days later. The Yak that he was sure he had downed earlier in the mission remained unconfirmed.

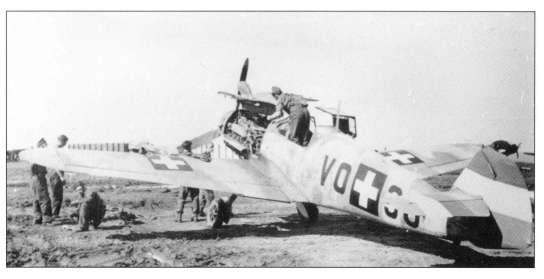

Fully marked up, a newly-delivered
Bf 109F-4 has its engine checked at
Ushin in late September 1943
*(Punka Archiv)*

When news of Debrődy's demise made it back to 5/2 FS, the unit immediately scrambled further aircraft, led by Lt Lajos Tóth, to search for the missing ace. During the course of the mission Russian fighters were spotted and the Hungarians immediately attacked. Tóth fired at a Yak-1 and saw it spiral into the ground, but he and his squadronmates were forced to flee when further Soviet fighters arrived on the scene.

Thirteen days later Cpl/Maj István Fábián and Sgt Károly Kereki were part of a patrol led by Lt Tóth that flew beyond the Dnieper Bend and deep into enemy territory. About 40 kms beyond the frontline the pilots attacked 30 Il-2s, two of which were downed by Tóth, while Fábián and Kereki claimed one apiece. These kills made both Tóth and Fábián aces.

In early October Soviet forces pushed on with their offensive, moving in the direction of Kiev. More air battles would follow, and during yet another engagement Lajos Tóth was shot down. Like Debrődy, he avoided being captured by swimming across the Dnieper.

On the 7th Lt László Molnár downed his fourth, fifth and sixth kills, the first of these being claimed when he and Miklós Kenyeres attacked four La-5s over the Dnieper Bend. As Kenyeres fired on one of the enemy fighters to the right of the formation, Molnár found himself face-to-face with the leading Soviet pilot, who had by then turned into the attacking

One of the 'Pumas'' last surviving
Bf 109F-4s taxies in at Ushin after an
aerial engagement in the early
autumn of 1943 *(Punka Archiv)*

Lt László Molnár of 5/2 FS belly-landed Bf 109G-6 V-3+84 at Varvasovka, in the Soviet Union, during the summer of 1943 (*Punka Archiv*)

Visible within this aircraft graveyard 'somewhere in Russia' is Hungarian Bf 109G V-3+44. Note also the upturned Fw 190 and propellerless Ju 87 (*Terray via Punka*)

Lt Kálmán Szeverényi poses astride the wheel of his white winter-camouflaged Bf 109G-1. Szeverényi was recalled to Hungary after scoring his first victory in October 1943, and he would claim four more while helping to defend his homeland (*Terray via Punka*)

Bf 109s. Turning his attention to the lead La-5, Molnár fired a burst in its direction and the pilot banked away to the east. The Hungarian hauled in the fleeing Lavochkin and continued to fire until it fell away in flames.

Later that day Molnár and Sgt Kovács were escorting a formation of bombers when they tangled with Russian fighters, which they soon drove off. Molnár then spotted a lone La-5 below them, heading east above the shimmering Dnieper. Diving down to 800 m, he bounced the enemy machine from astern and the Lavochkin burst into flames and hit the ground near the river's eastern bank. His sixth kill (an unidentified type) followed moments later when he again used the advantage of height to attack an unsuspecting target over the Bend. That same day also saw Lt Kenyeres claim two La-5 victories.

Another ace to enjoy success on the 7th was Lt Kálmán Szeverényi, who downed the first of his five victories when he too claimed an La-5. His kill was a little unusual, however, for he had just settled into a firing position behind the Lavochkin when the Russian pilot, who was unaware of the Hungarian's presence, spotted the Bf 109 whilst performing a gentle turn. He immediately bailed out without Szeverényi even firing a single shot! The Russian pilot landed near the wreckage of his aircraft.

In early November the 'Puma' group's field journal published a summary of its successes. The group had completed a total of 1560 missions up to the end of October. Of these, 5/I FG Staff had flown 81 and 5/1 FS 787. The rest of the missions were undertaken by 5/2 FS. Its aerial victory tally stood at 71, with 39 tons of bombs having been dropped.

On 1 November troops of the 1st Ukrainian Front launched an attack

Spare parts for the 'Pumas' are unloaded at a frontline airfield. Note the spinner among the boxes on the lorry. With Soviet aircraft roaming the skies in ever increasing numbers, such vehicles ran the risk of being strafed if they attempted to move during the hours of daylight *(Terray via Punka)*

from the Bukrin bridgehead, south of Kiev, to distract Axis attention away from the northern sector, where the main thrust was taking place.

Soviet air activity was hampered by bad weather until 3 November, when the sky became alive – the Soviet 2nd Air Army flew 1150 sorties during the course of the day. Shortly after midnight on the 6th, the red flag was raised over Kiev. The Hungarians retreated to Zhitomir later that day, and within the week had moved west to Kalinovka. On the 15th German troops began a counter-attack to try to recapture Kiev, but it failed.

They had better luck on the 20th, retaking Zhitomir, and the Hungarian pilots who had been mostly inactive because of bad weather returned to their former airfield. Despite the weather conditions, and the amount of relocating they had had to do, the 'Pumas' still claimed eight kills.

For much of December the Germans were kept busy making good their losses, while the Red Army prepared to launch a series of new attacks. Sorties continued, as both the air power and self-confidence of the enemy steadily increased. By the end of the year the number of aircraft within each Soviet close-support and fighter group had risen to 40.

December was also the month when the 'Pumas' notched up their 100th victory. Since their first mission, out of the original 37 pilots six had been lost in air combat while two had been listed as missing.

By the beginning of 1944 only 5/2 FS remained in the east. Within its modest ranks, the unit included a number of pilots from 5/1 FS whose tours of duty had not been completed when the unit pulled out. During the first weeks of the new year, Capt József Kovács gradually took over command of the squadron from Capt Horváth, who had been sent back to Hungary for a rest. The fighter sorties continued in January, and on the 5th Lt Debrödy claimed his 11th kill when he shot down an La-5.

Three days later the unit moved to Khalinovka. Whilst en route to their new base, Lt Molnár and wingman Cpl/Maj Ernő Kiss spotted 30 Il-2s flying towards the Hungarian lines. Above them, ten La-5s were providing cover. Despite being outnumbered 20-to-1, the Axis pilots engaged the enemy over Sugachova. A fierce fight broke out, with the Russians determined to reach their target, but unable to shake off the Hungarians.

Taking advantage of the escort fighters' late intervention, Lt Molnár quickly shot down three Il-2s to take his overall score into double figures. Defending his leader, Cpl/Maj Kiss then engaged an La-5 which was trying to get into a firing position behind Molnár. Kiss let off a burst and the Lavochkin fell away in flames. He now turned his attention to an Il-2.

Aces Lt László Molnár (left) and Lt Lajos Tóth are decorated with the Iron Cross, First Class, by German officers. Molnár received his award for shooting down three Il-2s and an La-5 on 8 January 1944, whilst Tóth was decorated for his leadership of 5/2 FS on the Eastern Front in 1943-44. The latter pilot achieved ten victories over the USSR and a further 16 in the skies over Hungary *(Punka Archiv)*

Lt László Molnár sits in the cockpit of Bf 109G-6 'Black 66' at Kalinovka, in the Soviet Union, in early 1944. Although the code V-66 had been assigned to the *Gustav*, there had only been time to paint on the numerals 66. Featuring the name *Erzsike* (Betty) behind the canopy, this unusually camouflaged fighter was used by Molnár to claim his 17th kill in early February 1944 *(Punka Archiv)*

Getting into a good firing position, his rounds hit their intended target and the *Stormovik's* rear gunner fell silent, the barrel of his weapon pointing skywards to mark the gunner's demise. A short burst from Kiss's cannon punched holes in the Il-2's fuselage, and the machine slowed down and started streaming smoke from its engine. Dropping away to its left, the aircraft exploded when it hit the ground.

In the meantime, Molnár had downed an La-5 that had attempted to attack his wingman, thus taking his tally to 14 victories. His achievement that day was considered extraordinary, for no other Hungarian would achieve four kills in one mission.

During preparations for the winter-spring offensive, the Soviet Air Force had been given several tasks. Firstly, it was to maintain strategic air power; secondly, it was to co-operate with ground forces in offensive operations; and finally, it was to harass enemy transport routes and continue to perform aerial reconnaissance missions. In order to fulfil these duties, aircrew were reinforced in frontline divisions, which consisted of three or four wings, and aircraft numbers in each wing increased to 40.

Involving more than 4000 aircraft, the campaign that was launched at the end of December 1943 and continued until the middle of April 1944 became one of the greatest battles of World War 2. On 1 January the forces of the 1st, 2nd and 3rd Ukrainian Fronts possessed 2600 aircraft, while *Luftflotte* 4 had 1460.

On 10 January Vinnitsa, which had at one stage been the Germans' Eastern Front headquarters, fell to the Russians. The breakthrough by the Red Army created a huge gap in the Axis defences, and the German Supreme Command threw in more and more troops to try to stop the attack. Counter-offensives against the advancing Red Army north of Uman and east of Vinnitsa were supported by air power, the Hungarians being airborne almost daily protecting bombers or flying fighter sorties.

On the 11th Lt Debrödy downed an Il-2 and an La-5 for his 12th and 13th victories. He was never short of targets in early 1944, for the Soviet air forces took to the air some 4200 times during this period. In mid January the Soviet advance slowed down, as communist troops waited for reinforcements. However, the work rate of its airmen did not diminish, with numerous close-support aircraft constantly attacking Hungarian airfields. Lt Molnár was one of a handful of 'Puma' pilots defending these bases, and by month-end he had boosted his tally to 16 kills.

Lt Debrődy was also heavily involved fighting the Soviets during this period, downing a Yak-1 on 25 January and an La-5 48 hours later. During the course of the month he flew 28 sorties – 25 fighter patrols, two bomber escorts and a solitary reconnaissance mission. Debrődy engaged enemy aircraft 11 times during these missions, claiming six kills (taking his tally to 15). He also force-landed in friendly territory.

Debrődy's great rival, Lt László Molnár, flew his 75th mission at the end of January, and early the

Lt László Molnár's Bf 109G-6 'Black 66' is seen in flight during an escort mission from its base at Kalinovka in early 1944 *(Punka Archiv)*

following month added two more kills to his tally. He was duly decorated with the Knights Cross of the Hungarian Order of Merit, before returning to Hungary with several other pilots. Meanwhile, 5/2 FS moved to Uman.

Soviet communiqués reported heavy air fighting during this period, aircraft of the 1st and 2nd Ukrainian Fronts flying 2800 combat sorties between 29 January and 3 February.

On 1 February Lts Kenyeres and Debrődy were given the job of escorting German Ju 52/3ms heading for the Khorsun-Shevchenkovsk salient with much needed supplies for the embattled troops on the ground. The duo were on their way home when Yak-9s and La-5s bounced them from above. Debrődy immediately went on the attack, despite being unable to talk with his wingman due to radio failure. During the ensuing melée, Kenyeres became separated from his leader, leaving him unprotected.

Debrődy soon shot down an La-5, but was then hit himself. With his engine misfiring and smoke filling the cockpit, the ace jettisoned the canopy and prepared to abandon the machine when he noticed his height on the altimeter. Debrődy was too low to bail out. Left with no other choice than to belly-land in Russian territory, he strapped himself back into his seat and successfully set his machine down in a field. Angered by the apparent loss of his leader, Kenyeres avenged his colleague by shooting down the victorious Yak-9, thus taking his own tally to 18 kills. This success made him the leading Hungarian ace at the time.

Pilots of 5/2 FS take part in a last minute briefing at Kalinovka before departing on a mission in early 1944. Lt László Molnár was flying from this base when he scored four kills in just one day (on 9 January) to earn him the Iron Cross, First Class. This feat made him the leading Hungarian ace at the time. Notice the groundcrewman on the wing of the Bf 109, adding the finishing touches to a white Hungarian cross *(Mátyás via Punka)*

On the ground, Debrődy had staggered out of his aircraft just as Russian soldiers started to run towards him across the field. The Hungarian ace immediately set about destroying the radio and other vital equipment in his wrecked aircraft. From above, Kenyeres could clearly see the white-crossed fighter and the approaching troops. Realising the predicament Debrődy was in, he acted instinctively. 'I did not think about what I was doing until the landing gear was down', he

This 5/2 FS Bf 109G-2/R6 is seen soon after receiving its Hungarian codes and crosses *(Papp)*

later explained. Debrődy heard the roar of an incoming aircraft, and he was astonished to see Kenyeres coming in to land. Fortunately, the ground was relatively flat (and covered in 15 cms of snow), and Kenyeres landed without any problems 180 m from Debrődy.

By then the ace was sprinting towards the *Gustav*. The cockpit of the Bf 109 was small even for one person, let alone two, so Kenyeres jettisoned the canopy, leapt out and discarded his parachute. Both pilots tore off their heavy winter jackets and Debrődy clambered into the cockpit. Jumping into the seat, he put his feet on the rudder pedals while Kenyeres sat on his lap, grabbed the control column and shoved the throttle lever all the way forward. By now the Russian soldiers were getting within firing range, and bullets began whizzing by and mortar shells exploded around them. With the Messerschmitt thundering down the field, Kenyeres spotted a shallow trench directly in their path, so he eased off the throttle. The aircraft shuddered, sped over the obstacle and then became airborne.

The two friends flew back to Uman, huddling behind the armoured windshield that provided little protection against the bitter cold.

Two days later, in an ironic twist of fate, the left wing of Kenyeres' Messerschmitt was hit and he had to bail out over a dense forest. This time the terrain was not suitable for landing, and Debrődy could only circle helplessly above his friend. Remaining in the area until his fuel got so low that he ran out approaching the frontline, Debrődy was forced to make an emergency landing within site of Soviet territory. Despite Kenyeres being captured, both aces were able to resume their friendship post-war, and this lasted until Debrődy's death in 1984.

Mechanics work on a DB 605 engine hoisted up by a tripod crane *(Punka Archiv)*

Aces Tóth and Molnár are flanked by two unknown pilots in Russia in early 1944 *(Punka Archiv)*

On 16 February Debrődy sortied from Uman and claimed his 17th and 18th victories when he downed two Il-2s. He had now equalled Miklós Kenyeres tally.

Despite the constant retreating, the 'Pumas' were still fighting over Kiev itself. Up to now they had encountered only Soviet or British-built aircraft, but now they also found themselves face-to-face with American-built machines. Notori-

It may not have had the same performance as a Bf 109, but this mud-spattered sedan carried the same 'Puma' emblem as most 5/I FG machines in 1943-44 *(Terray via Punka)*

This photograph of 5/2 FS's Bf 109G-3/R6 V.3+27 having its engine worked on was taken at the same time as the tripod crane shot opposite. Note that the fighter's fuselage and wing crosses have been overpainted to render the *Gustav* less conspicuous both in the air and on the ground *(Terray via Punka)*

ously difficult to shoot down, the P-39, in particular, was a highly prized scalp, and Lt Tóth managed to down one – for his tenth kill – on 27 February near Kirowograd.

5/2 FS scored some 50 victories in the first two months of 1944, during which time, according to *Luftflotte* 4 reports, the Hungarians had received 66 Bf 109s.

March brought no respite for the unit, with 5/2 FS moving from Uman to Khalinovka on the 1st, and then retreating west to Proshkhurov the following day. Two weeks later the squadron was pulled out of the frontline.

On 19 March the Germans virtually occupied Hungary.

At this time an aircraft shortage caused by the rapid Soviet advance led to the withdrawal of 5/2 FS to Zamoshch-Mokre airfield. Although short of Bf 109s, the unit continued to welcome new pilots, who completed their training on the few fighters available to 5/2 FS. Once cleared for combat, their primary task was to escort Hungarian and German Ju 88s. According to stories at the time, there were frequent disagreements between the inexperienced fighter pilots and the bomber crews, the latter taking a dim view of the tactics employed by their Hungarian escorts.

The latter would usually fly between 500 m and 1000 m above the bombers to prevent enemy fighters from making use of any height advantage. However, the Soviet pilots avoided the fighter escorts by approaching from lower altitudes, and on several occasions the Hungarians did not even realise that their charges were under attack! By the time they

Lt Lajos Tóth of the 5/2 FS poses with his Bf 109G-6 V-3+73 at Uman, in the Soviet Union, in early 1944 (*Punka Archiv*)

responded to the bombers' calls for help the enemy had disappeared. German fighter pilots, on the other hand, flew close behind and above their charges to provide adequate cover. The bomber crews thus preferred to fly with German escorts.

Changeable weather during the second half of March frequently kept the fighters on the ground until month-end. Most of the missions that they did manage to fly involved patrolling over the Polish towns of Brody and, from the beginning of April, Luck. Later in the month fighters covered formations sent to bomb targets near Kovel, in the Ukraine. It was on one of the latter sorties that Capt József Kovács downed an Il-2, the veteran pilot completing his 100th combat mission at the end of April – this event was well publicised by German and Hungarian war correspondents.

As a result of its frequent moves northwards, 5/2 FS was placed under the command of *Luftflotte* 6. It was also given a new name – 102 Independent Fighter Squadron – but it had few aircraft left, and there was talk of its possible repatriation. But this uncertainty did not stop missions being flown, with the unit mostly escorting Ju 87s. A typical flight in early June saw six fighters of 102/1 FS receive orders to protect German and Hungarian Stukas. The dive-bombers' goal was to disrupt enemy vehicle traffic which had been reported by reconnaissance crews to be moving south-east of Mielec. Ten minutes after the fighters took off, the Stukas appeared over the rendezvous area. After exchanging greetings over the radio, the fighters took up position above and below the Ju 87s.

Captured on camera, Capt József Kovács, CO of 102/1 FS, returns from his 100th mission at the end of April 1944. This outstanding achievement was celebrated in newsreels shown both in Hungary and in Germany. Capt Kovács scored four kills on the Eastern Front, his final victory (an Il-2 shot down during a bomber escort mission) being claimed just days prior to him reaching his century (*Vági via Petrick*)

Soviet flak gunners put up a barrage, with black 'pom-poms' exploding at 1500 m. Once over the target, the lead Stuka pilot pushed over into a dive and the others followed him in single file. The fighters, meanwhile, remained above and waited for the dive-bombing to end. Suddenly, enemy

fighters appeared in amongst the thin clouds, and one of the Hungarian flights, led by future five-kill ace Lt Kálmán Szeverényi, turned to face the Soviet fighters. Szeverényi's initial burst of fire missed its target, so he pulled up and looked down to see what was happening to the Stukas they were protecting. Seconds later rounds from a Soviet fighter whizzed past his cockpit, so Szeverényi dived into cloud in an attempt to lose his attacker. Emerging behind his foe, he was just about to engage the enemy when a second fighter latched onto his tail, forcing him to break away.

Attempting to evade the fighter behind him, the Hungarian heard a loud bang as his Messerschmitt was hit, but it did not distract him for long. He eventually succeeded in getting astern of his opponent, and he hit the fighter with both machine gun and cannon rounds. Ten minutes after landing, Szeverényi received Capt Kovács' congratulations. His victory was confirmed by ground troops and his wingman.

On 6 June a second Hungarian fighter squadron arrived at the front. Having previously been based at Kolozsvár conducting fighter training and anti-aircraft defence roles on *Héjas*, 102/2 FS immediately commenced its conversion onto the Bf 109. A month later the unit went into action led by veteran pilot, and future 13-kill ace, 1/Lt László Pottyondy.

102/1 and 102/2 FSs would spend much of their brief existence retreating in the face of the rapidly advancing Red Army. On 22 July 102/2 FS pulled back to Reichshof. It did not stay here long, however, retreating just two days later to Mielec and then to Balitze on 27 July. 102/1 FS, meanwhile, moved to the airfield at Deblin-Irena on the 24th. Under these circumstances, it was not possible to carry out combat flights.

By the early autumn the situation had changed significantly. The Soviet Army stood before the Hungarian frontier, at the passes of the Carpathian Mountains. To the south the Germans were in constant retreat due to Rumania changing sides in August. Holding the frontlines became impossible, so almost all Hungarian flying units on the Eastern Front were pulled back to bases in Hungary itself. 102/1 FS was transferred to Munkács (now Munkachevo), and from here pilots carried out numerous missions attacking Soviet aircraft which were supporting the Red Army's advance towards the north-eastern mountain passes through the Carpathians.

**Precariously propped up on four ammunition boxes, V-3+80 prepares to have its guns tested. The fighter lacks the Hungarian red-white-green marking on its tail** *(Punka Archiv)*

**Bf 109G-6 V-3+81 in a familiar pose. The combination of tricky take off and landing characteristics and a notoriously weak undercarriage meant that more Bf 109s were written off in accidents than were shot down by the Allies in World War 2 *(Punka Archiv)***

It was in this area, near Shanok, on 13 September that Capt Kovács downed an Il-2. The following day there was a fierce engagement again over Shanok. Ens István Kálmán was on his way to Munkács when he shot down a Soviet observation balloon spying on Hungarian troops that were working on fortifications to defend one of the passes. Minutes later German and Hungarian troops were attacked by Il-2s and Yak-9s, and Capt Kovács, Ens Kálmán, 1/Lt Máthé and Cpl/Maj Csikós rushed to their aid. In the brief dogfight which ensued, each of the pilots brought down a *Stormovik* – these were the first kills for future aces Kálmán and Máthé. The Soviet formation was pursued home by the Hungarians as far as Krosno, where Capt Kovács added to the list of kills by downing an Il-2 and a Yak-9. Twenty-four hours later 1/Lt Pottyondy, commander of 102/2 FS, shot down an Il-2 near Mezdilaborze.

Although the advancing Red Army was stopped at the Eastern Carpathians, German and Hungarian forces could not hold back the Soviet attack which was launched on Transylvania. Axis forces lost many perfectly serviceable aircraft as a handful of airfields were captured, and many more machines were written off during the rapid retreat.

In October one of the greatest tank battles of World War 2 was fought to capture Debrecen. During the engagement, which lasted almost three weeks, numerous Luftwaffe aircraft were committed to the protection of ground forces. Meanwhile, 102/1 and 102/2 FSs, which were based nearby, were moved from Munkács to Felsőábrány and ordered to fly missions against Soviet supply lines. The battle at Debrecen, which involved several hundred tanks, ended with a Soviet victory on 20 October. German and Hungarian troops were forced into retreat yet again.

On the 21st both units were pulled back to Ferihegy, where they flew missions for another month. During this time more kills were scored over Soviet aircraft supporting the Red Army advance across the Great Plain.

Whilst at Ferihegy 1/Lt Pottyondy was promoted to captain, and the group moved to Budaörs soon afterwards. Before long 102/1 FS was pulled back to Inota, near Várpalota, and 102/2 FS to Bábolnapuszta. near Győr. From October, the group's history was interwoven with that of the 'Pumas'. On 23 February 1945 Kovács, now a major, compiled the following report about the activities of 102/1 and 102/2 FSs;

'Between 1 January and 31 December 1944 102/1 FS flew 1339 missions and spent 1646 hours over enemy territory. It downed 67 aircraft and two observation balloons, and destroyed 17 trucks, one fuel truck and an armoured reconnaissance car. The unit lost six pilots and 12 aircraft in action and 33 to mechanical failures. Between 7 July and 31 December 1944 102/2 FS flew 334 missions and spent 309 hours over enemy territory. It downed 18 aircraft and destroyed a tank. The unit lost three pilots and seven aircraft in action and 18 to mechanical failure.'

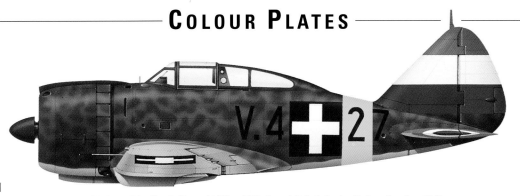

**1**
Re.2000 *Heja* V.4+27 of Lt Imre Páncél, 1/1 'Dongó' (Wasp) FS, Staryj Oskol, Soviet Union, October 1942

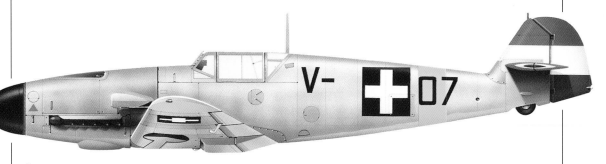

**2**
Bf 109F-4/B V-+07 of Sgt Dezső Szentgyörgyi, 1/1 FS, Rossosh, Soviet Union, early 1943

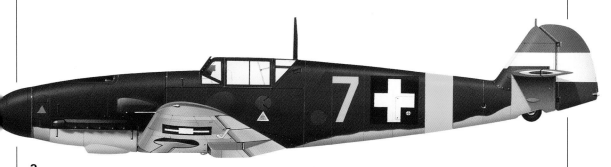

**3**
Bf 109F-4/B 'Yellow 7' of Sgt Dezső Szentgyörgyi, 1/1 FS, Poltava, Soviet Union, late February 1943

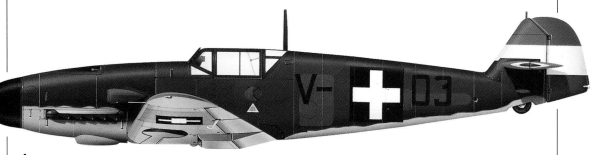

**4**
Bf 109F-4/B V-+03 of 1/Lt György Debrődy, 5/1 FS, Uman, Soviet Union, Spring 1943

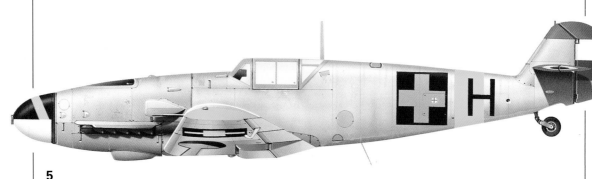

**5**
Bf 109G-2 'Black H' of Lt Kálmán Szeverényi, 5/2 FS, Soviet Union, Spring 1943

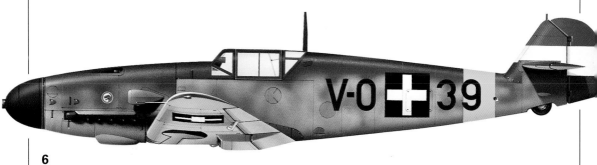

**6**
Bf 109F-4/B V-0+39 of Maj Aladár Heppes, Group Commander of 5/I FG, Kharkov, Soviet Union, May 1943

**7**
Bf 109F-4/B V.0+41 of Sgt Pál Kovács, 5/2 FS, Varvasovka, Soviet Union, Summer 1943

**8**
Bf 109G-6 V-3+84 of Lt László Molnár, 5/2 FS, Varvasovka, Soviet Union, August 1943

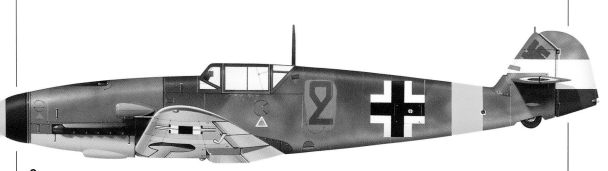

**9**
Bf 109F-4 'Red 2' of Sgt/Maj Dezső Szentgyörgyi, 1/1 FS, Kursk-East, Soviet Union, late 1943

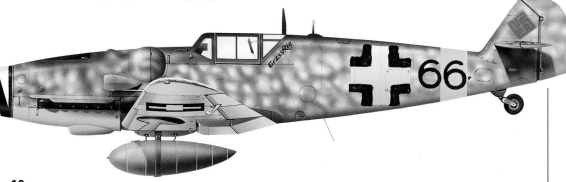

**10**
Bf 109G-6 'Black 66' of Lt László Molnár, 5/2 FS, Kalinovka, Soviet Union, early 1944

**11**
Bf 109G-6 V3+73 of Lt Lajos Tóth, 5/2 FS, Uman, Soviet Union, February 1944

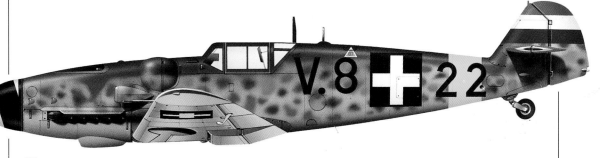

**12**
Bf 109G-6 V.8+22 of 1/Lt Pál Irányi, First Officer of 101/I 'Puma' FG, Veszprém, Hungary, May 1944

**13**
Bf 109G-6 (Gy.sz. 95 226) V.8+10 of Maj Aladár Heppes, Group Commander of 101/I FG, Veszprém, Hungary, May 1944

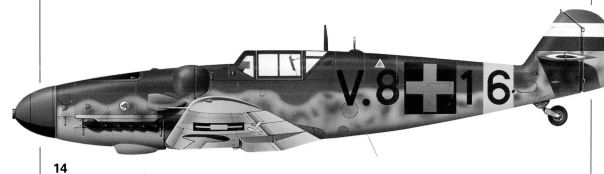

**14**
Bf 109G-6 (Gy.sz. 95 244) V.8+16 of 1/Lt József Bejczy, 101/3 'Puma' FS, Veszprém, Hungary, Summer 1944

**15**
Bf 109G-6 V.8+48 of Lt László Molnár, 101/3 'Puma' FS, Veszprém, Hungary, July 1944

**16**
Bf 109G-6 V.8+53 of Lt Mihály Karátsonyi, 101/3 'Puma' FS, Veszprém, Hungary, Summer 1944

**17**
Bf 109G-6/U2 W-0+20 of Sgt Mátyás Lörincz, 101/2 'Puma' FS, Veszprém, Hungary, Summer 1944

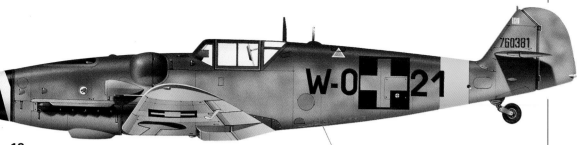

**18**
Bf 109G-6/U2 (Wk-Nr 760381) W-0+21 of Lt László Dániel, 101/3 'Puma' FS, Veszprém, Hungary, Summer 1944

**19**
Bf 109G-6/U2 W-0+49 of Lt Kálmán Nánási, 101/3 'Puma' FS, Veszprém, Hungary, Summer 1944

**20**
Bf 109G-6/U2 W-0+70 of 1/Lt Pál Irányi, First Officer of 101/I 'Puma' FG, Veszprém, Hungary, Summer 1944

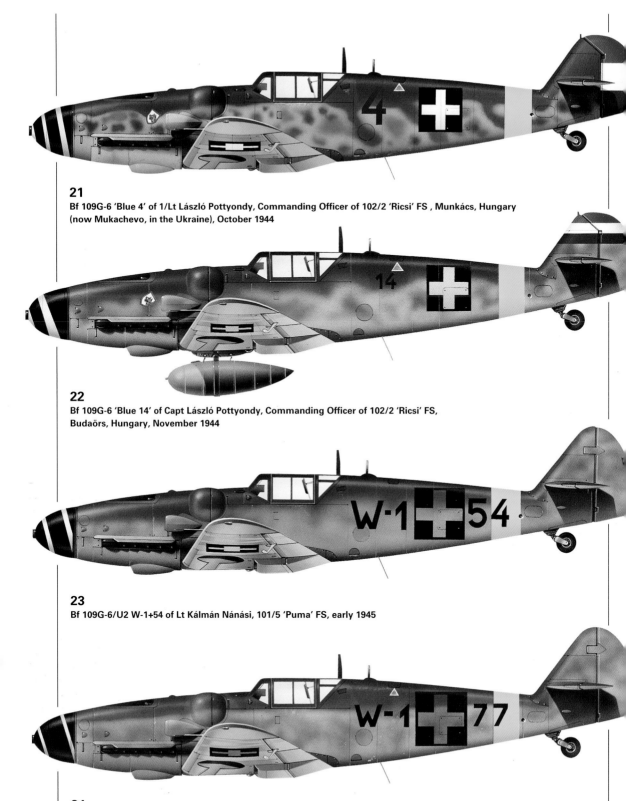

**21**
Bf 109G-6 'Blue 4' of 1/Lt László Pottyondy, Commanding Officer of 102/2 'Ricsi' FS , Munkács, Hungary (now Mukachevo, in the Ukraine), October 1944

**22**
Bf 109G-6 'Blue 14' of Capt László Pottyondy, Commanding Officer of 102/2 'Ricsi' FS, Budaörs, Hungary, November 1944

**23**
Bf 109G-6/U2 W-1+54 of Lt Kálmán Nánási, 101/5 'Puma' FS, early 1945

**24**
Bf 109G-6/U2 W-1+77 of Ens Dezső Szentgyörgyi, 101/2 'Puma' FS, Veszprém, Hungary, January 1945

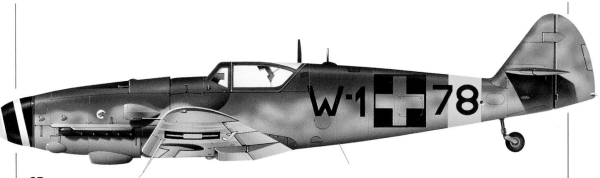

**25**
Bf 109G-10 W-1+78 of Cpl/Maj Lajos Krascsenics, 101/3 'Puma' FS, Veszprém, Hungary, early 1945

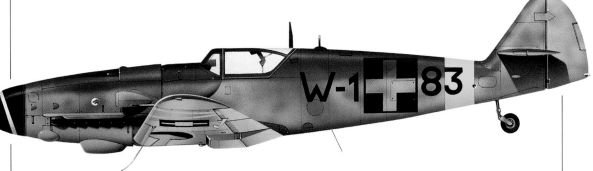

**26**
Bf 109G-10 W-1+83 of Lt László Dániel, 101/3 'Puma' FS, Veszprém, Hungary, early 1945

**27**
Bf 109G-6/U2 W-1+44 of Lt György Michna, 101/1 'Puma' FS, Veszprém, Hungary, February 1945

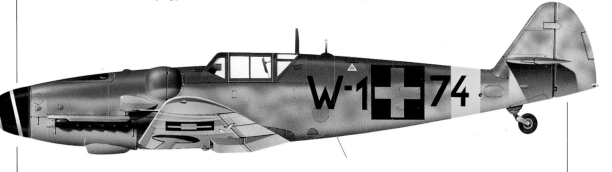

**28**
Bf 109G-6/U2 W-1+74 of Sgt/Maj István Fábián, 101/2 'Puma' FS, Veszprém, Hungary, February 1945

**29**
Bf 109G-6/U2 W-1+71 of Lt József Málik, 101/2 'Puma' FS, Veszprém, Hungary, 9 March 1945

**30**
Bf 109G-10/U4 (Wk-Nr 613107) 'Yellow 5' of Ens István Fábián, 101/2 'Puma' FS , Veszprém, Hungary, March 1945

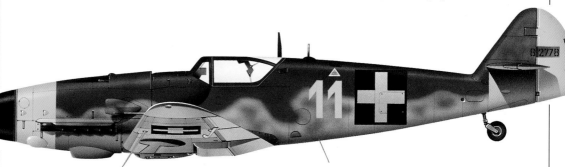

**31**
Bf 109G-10/U4 (Wk-Nr 612778) 'Yellow 11' of Ens István Fábián, 101/2 'Puma' FS, Raffelding, Austria,
10 April 1945

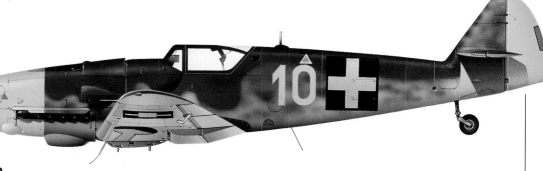

**32**
Bf 109G-10/U4 'Yellow 10' of Cpl/Maj Ernö Kiss, 101/III 'Puma' FG, Raffelding, Austria, April 1945

# HOME DEFENCE

A look at the political situation in Hungary from early 1943 onwards will help to explain the expansion of the air force, and within it the creation of Bf 109-equipped units for home defence.

The defeat of the 2nd Hungarian Army at Voronezh in January 1943 made it obvious to government figures loyal to Adm Horthy that Germany's complete defeat by the Anglo-American-Soviet alliance was unavoidable. The terrible losses of 1943 had enabled the Hungarian government to withdraw its troops, or what was left of them, from the Eastern Front without German permission. Now, only a few poorly armed divisions and one air force brigade, consisting of six squadrons (two of which were fighter units), remained at the front. The number of squadrons had been further reduced to four by the end of 1943.

At the same time Hungarian government officials, through diplomatic channels in neutral countries, contacted their counterparts in Britain and the US and tried to convince them that the only reason they had entered the war against the Allies was to achieve 'border revision', not because they were supporting Hitler's war, and that they were ready to sign an armistice. On 10 October 1943, after lengthy, and secret, negotiations, Hungary, the US and Britain signed a preliminary armistice agreement in the Portuguese capital Lisbon, with the condition that it would come into force when the Allies reached the Hungarian border. The Hungarian government fully expected an Anglo-American landing in the Balkans.

Twelve months earlier, the Axis powers had been occupying the largest area of the USSR and North Africa that they would hold at any time during the war. However, Soviet night attacks on 4 September 1942 proved that some communist aircraft could still reach Budapest with a limited bomb load. Although such attacks seemed insignificant from a military point of view, they raised a number of issues.

Firstly, Budapest's flak defences were inadequate, with the accuracy of the few weapons available being poor. Secondly, its air raid system left much to be desired. Thirdly, on many occasions the raiders used the city's lights and radio stations for navigation. Finally, the Soviet bombers were never once intercepted by Hungarian nightfighters.

As a result of these problems, on 1 October 1942 plans were formulated that would see three fighter groups assigned to home defence (not including the units on the Eastern Front) during 1943. It was proposed that 5/I FG should be based in Budapest, 1 FG at Szolnok and 2 FG at Kolozsvr (now Cluj). These groups were also to be enlarged from two to three squadrons.

As it turned out, 5/I FG was sent to the Eastern Front and its place was taken at Mtysfld airfield, near Budapest, by 2/1 FS, which had been recalled from the USSR. After March 1943 this was the only fighter unit based in Hungary that was available for home defence. Not that its presence amounted to much, for the squadron was equipped with the last surviving Re.2000 *Hejas*, which would have offered little opposition to attacking allied forces.

43

**Hidden talents. Unlike many Axis fighter units, the 'Pumas'' distinctive marking was applied in such a way as to be almost invisible. This combat-weary Bf 109G-6 is typically marked** *(Tobak via Punka)*

Later in the year the unit moved to Ferihegy, where 5/1 Experimental Night Fighter Squadron (NFS) was also stationed, along with other Hungarian and German units. The squadron was equipped with 18 *Hejas*, including reserve aircraft.

When the Hungarian Minister of Defence, Col Gen Lajos Csatay, reviewed the military preparedness of his nation in mid 1943, he stated, 'We have 50 *Heja* aircraft at the present time. However, these are no match for American Liberator bombers. They can only be used as training machines in future'.

Replacement of the Re.2000s was near, for the Hungarian Railway Carriage and Engineering Works (MWG) was in the process of gearing up to licence-build Bf 109G-4/6s in Győr. Some 92 had been delivered by the end of 1943.

Some of these new aircraft were to be issued to 2/1 FS according to government defence plans, allowing the unit to be combat ready by November 1943 at the earliest. 5/3 FS was also to be re-equipped for use in the air defence role from spring 1944 onwards. The intention was to station this unit at Horthyliget airfield due to overcrowding at Ferihegy. Pilots for both units would come from 5/I Fighter Auxiliary Group (FAG), whose nine Bf 109s would in turn be thrown into action only in case of emergency. Hungarian pilots returning from training in Börgönd, near Szkésfehérvár, and those transferred back from the Eastern Front (ex-5/2 FS) would receive conversion training onto the Bf 109G with 5/I FAG.

Adding to this defensive strength was Bf 109-equipped 1/1 FS in Szolnok. Finally, whether needed or not, 1/2 Fighter Training Squadron, with 12 *Héjas*, was available from 1 February 1944 at Tapolca.

In comparison to the planned strength outlined above, the actual strength of National Air Defence Command was as follows – from 1 February 1944, 2/1 FS was at Ferihegy, 1/1 FS, from 1 April 1944, was at Szolnok, and 5/3 FS, from 1 May 1944, was also at Ferihegy. Each unit was equipped with 18 Hungarian-built Bf 109Gs.

From January 1944 onwards, British and US flights over Hungary became routine. By the following month, 2/1 FS, led by Capt Miklós Scholtz, had received 20 Bf 109Gs, and its pilots had gained the necessary experience to fly them in combat. Although no such missions were flown in February, the training of 1/1 FS continued at Szolnok.

By March 1944, Hungary's war situation had deteriorated still further. The Red Army had reached the frontier at the north-east Carpathians, and Hitler, who now knew about the Hungarian government's plan to quit the war, had ordered the German occupation of the country. This took place on 19 March, after which a new, pro-German, government was established. Political opposition was banned, and senior positions were filled by officers with German sympathies. The 1st Army, which had been held in reserve, was immediately mobilised and sent to the Carpathians.

After a 12-month lull, Hungarian troops faced Soviet forces once again. Hungary could no longer count on Anglo-American tolerance.

In the immediate wake of the German occupation of Hungary, the Royal Hungarian Air Force had been banned from taking to the air. However, once the Germans became confident that it would remain loyal, they allowed its pilots to fly combat sorties again.

One of the first missions flown following the lifting of the ban took place on 17 March, when 12 fighters from 2/1 FS were scrambled to attack an incoming bombing raid – the only one that month. Air raid sirens had sounded at noon, and from the south-west, 70 unescorted four-engined aircraft approached over Lake Balaton. The formation turned towards Budapest, and 2/1 FS took off. The 1st Flight was led by Capt Miklós Scholtz, the 2nd Flight by the unit's First Officer (and future ace), 1/Lt Pál Irányi, and the 3rd Flight by 1/Lt Elemér Szombathelyi. Within minutes of taking off the unit was ordered to return by 'Rock Centre', the code name for the Hungarian Fighter Control Centre. The controllers believed the fighters had taken off without auxiliary tanks!

However, due to radio trouble contact was not made with the 3rd Flight, who clashed with the Americans over Lake Velence. The USAAF B-24s, flying in a tight formation, put up a formidable concentration of fire, and the four Hungarians, lacking experience in dealing with American tactics, approached them from the wrong direction and got in too close before opening fire. All four Bf 109s were hit and two went down.

Cpl István Kis-Benedek was killed when he crashed 15 kms from Szabadhidvég. Sgt János Murvay also died when his fighter hit a house and exploded whilst attempting an emergency landing near Mezőkomárom. 1/Lt Szombathelyi and Lt Miklós Molnár made it back to base, having scored hits on two B-24s. None had been downed though.

The USAAF returned again on 3 April when about 180 four-engined bombers and 170 fighters of the Fifteenth Air Force attacked Budapest. Their targets were the Ferencvçros marshalling yard, the oil refineries on Csepel Island and the Dunai aircraft factory, which was licence-producing the Me 210. Due to poor aiming, some of the bombs fell on non-military targets, including a hospital, leaving 1073 dead and 526 wounded.

Most Hungarians believed that the attack was a result of the German occupation and the creation of the pro-German government, but this was not the case. A list of Hungarian targets, and a timetable for attacks, had been agreed by the Allies at the Teheran Conference in November 1943.

2/1 FS, led by 1/Lt Irányi, had attempted to defend Budapest on the 3rd. The spring weather was good when the pilots took off at 1000 hrs, but they were recalled by 'Rock Centre' 35 minutes later. Five minutes after landing they were scrambled again, although most of the Bf 109s were kept away from the bombers by the large number of US fighters.

1/1 FS, led by 7-kill ace Capt György Ujszászy, was also sent into action from Szolnok for the first time on 3 April. Its pilots tried to join up with their comrades in 2/1 FS, but instead ran into a formation of unescorted Liberators. Attacking one of the bombers at the edge of the formation, Capt Ujszászy and Sgt Károly Kereki succeeded in bringing it down.

2/1 FS's 1/Lt Tibor Papp attacked a damaged Liberator which was flying along the River Danube towards the south, the bomber bursting into flames and crashed into the river at Kulcs. This kill took Papp's tally to four

Both aces and leaders, Lt György Debrődy (left) and 1/Lt Pál Irányi chat between sorties at Veszprém, in Hungary, in the spring of 1944. Irányi was among the first pilots to be retrained on the Bf 109, and he flew more than 100 combat missions. He commanded 101/I FG from October 1944 *(Irányi via Punka)*

kills, the pilot having claimed a trio of victories in the USSR in 1943. 2/1 FS pilots scored a total of four victories. One of these fell to 1/Lt Irányi, his B-17 force-landing north of Ferihegy. A test pilot from the Air Force Experimental Institute also claimed to have shot down a B-17 over Somorja.

The official military communiqué issued at the end of the day said 17 American aircraft had been brought down, six of them by flak. However, of the fighters' 11 'kills', only six were confirmed. It is believed that four of the latter were B-17s (42-31456, 42-30381, 42-30436 and 42-39986) and one was a B-24 (42-52322). In return, a single Hungarian pilot lost his life.

Whilst one groundcrewman checks on the well being of his pilot, a second prepares to hand-crank the DB 605 engine in his Bf 109G-6 into life. This photograph, of an aircraft from 2/1 FS, was taken at Ferihegy, in Hungary, prior to the devastating USAAF bombing raid on the airfield on 13 April 1944. Note the Hungarian-built Me 210s parked in the distance *(Vági via Petrick)*

At 1100 hrs on 13 April, several hundred USAAF bombers, escorted by P-38 Lightnings and P-47 Thunderbolts, entered Hungarian airspace. Ferihegy airfield and the Danube Aircraft Factory, south of Budapest, were the targets. This time the bombing was accurate, and many training aircraft at Ferihegy were destroyed. Hangars and workshops belonging to the Air Force's Experimental Institute were also hit, destroying both experimental aircraft and Me 210s alike.

Meanwhile, a formation of more than 160 bombers attacked MWG's Bf 109 assembly plant, and its airfield, at Győr, which was the most important facility of its kind in Hungary. Finally, a smaller formation of 48 B-17s bombed the powerplant at Bánhida.

Twelve Bf 109s of 2/1 FS were scrambled at 1100 hrs, the formation, led by Capt Scholtz, climbing up to intercept the raiders when they received the order to head to Győr. By the time they arrived over the factory the US bombers had dropped their ordnance and gone. 'Rock Centre' then ordered Bf 109s to Bánhida, where they again arrived too late.

Told to return to Ferihegy for refuelling, Capt Scholtz and the three members of his flight had just landed when Liberators appeared overhead. Cpl/Maj Kasza's Bf 109 was wrecked when a bomb exploded nearby, but he survived. The remaining three aircraft were undamaged.

1/Lt Irányi's flight was following close behind, the pilots having extended their gear and flaps when they were told to abort their landing and divert to another airfield. Irányi noticed a low-flying B-24 over Gödöllő and attacked, hitting its wing-root. The bomber exploded.

Besides the eight B-24s and six P-38s claimed by the Hungarian pilots on this day, flak batteries were also credited with six kills, including two P-47s near Budapest.

Following the attacks on Budapest and the raid on Győr, the USAAF believed that it had neutralised aircraft manufacturing in Hungary, and turned its attention to the Rumanian oil fields. Future operations in Hungarian airspace would be performed by the RAF, which conducted smaller-scale bombing raids at night, as well as the mining of the River Danube, codenamed Operation *Gardening*. However, American aircraft continued to fly through Hungarian airspace whilst implementing Operation *Frantic Joe* – the transportation of bombs, fuel and groundcrew from Italy to the Soviet Union.

Between 13 April and 24 May Hungarian fighters were scrambled several times, although they made no contact with the enemy. This respite was long enough for the National Home Defence Centre (NHDC) to set up 101 home defence Fighter Group (FG) as the first part of the planned 101 home defence Fighter Wing. Command of the group was assigned to Maj Aladár Heppes, the 'old Puma'. Now aged 40, and with four kills from 1943 to his credit, he was still very much a frontline fighter pilot.

With the formation of 101 FG, for the third time in World War 2 the famous 'Puma head' symbol appeared on aircraft assigned to the group's trio of squadrons. The formation of the third of these units – 5/3 FS – was accelerated to the point where it deployed on 1 May 1944.

The lengthy absence of American aircraft not only allowed the relocation of 5/3 FS, the Group Staff and the necessary ground support crew to the airfield at Veszprém-Jutas, it also meant that novice pilots got the chance to practise both formation flying and air-to-air gunnery. Finally, all three units also had the opportunity to work on new tactics.

The NHDC had realised that better co-ordination between the movement of the three squadrons was the only way to compensate for the enormous numerical superiority enjoyed by the Fifteenth Air Force. Attacking the bombers' 'box formations' required co-ordination, so the newly devised tactical plan called for a pair of fighters from one squadron to intercept a single bomber, while fighters from the other units protected them against USAAF escorts attacking from the flanks and from above.

As previously mentioned, 101 'Puma' FG was led by Maj Heppes, with Capt Gyula Horváth as his deputy. 101/1 FS (formerly 2/1 FS) was codenamed 'Zongora' (Piano), and it continued to be commanded by Capt Miklós Scholtz, with 1/Lt Pál Irányi as his First Officer. 101/2 FS (formerly 1/1 FS) was codenamed 'Retek' (Radish), and Capt György Ujszászy placed in charge. His first officer was 1/Lt János Kőhalmy. Finally, 101/3 FS (formerly 5/3 FS) was codenamed 'Drótkefe' (Wire Brush) and led by 1/Lt József Bejczy, with 1/Lt György Pávai-Vajna as First Officer.

Each squadron was equipped with 12 Bf 109Gs, which combined with Group Staff's four *Gustavs* to give 101 FG an overall strength of 40

This heavily mottled Hungarian-built Bf 109G-6 is seen at Veszprém in April 1944. Assigned to 101/3 FS, its Hungarian national markings have also been significantly toned down with grey overspray *(Punka Archiv)*

Veteran fighter pilot, and CO of 101/3 FS, Lt József Bejczy was shot down and killed on 4 November 1944 whilst attempting to attack Soviet tanks that he had dicovered hiding in haystacks near Szolnok *(Punka Archiv)*

aircraft, all of which could be in action at the same time. Although not a match for Allied fighter units in-theatre, 101 FG was nevertheless twice as large as the force that had intercepted USAAF formations in April and early May.

With 16 pilots per squadron, four men could be off duty each day. However, the units were issued with only two spare aircraft instead of the required four.

101/3 'Drótkefe' boasted the most experienced pilots of the three units within 101 FG, including leading aces Lts Debrődy and Molnár, both of whom had returned from the USSR with 18 victories apiece. Squadron commander 1/Lt Bejczy had also seen lengthy service on the Easter Front. 101/2 'Retek' also included two veteran 'Puma' pilots within its ranks, 10-kill ace 1/Lt Lajos Tóth and 6-kill ace Sgt Dezső Szentgyörgyi.

101 FG's first mission took place on 24 May, when 13 aircraft of 101/1 'Zongora' FS, led by Capt Scholtz, were scrambled to intercept a large formation of B-24s flying over the Dunántúl (Transdanubia – the area west of the Danube), bound for oil refineries near Vienna. The squadron took off at 1100 hrs and headed for Komárom, before being directed towards Wiener Neustadt. West of Sopron, Lt Lajos Benkő and his wingman Cpl/Maj József Nagy attacked an unescorted formation of B-24s and shot down a bomber each – both victims crash-landed on Austrian soil. Having used up most of their ammunition, the victorious Hungarian pilots landed at Veszprém.

Meanwhile, the rest of the squadron had attacked a scattered formation of B-17s and B-24s near Wiener Neustadt, Capt Scholtz claiming a B-17 and Cpl/Maj Kasza downing a B-24. 101/1 FS then attempted to regroup, but the unit was bounced by a larger force of P-51s. In the ensuing dogfight Capt Scholtz shot down a P-51, but Cpl/Maj Kasza was himself forced to bail out. Only three fighters made it back to Veszprém following this mission, the rest making emergency landings at other airfields in Hungary and Austria. Aside from Kasza, who landed safely in his parachute, the only other squadron loss was Lt Sándor Sárkány, who was shot down and killed whilst attacking a B-24 over Alsólendva.

Confirmed USAAF losses were one B-17, three B-24s and one P-51, with a second Liberator probably shot down. 101/1 FS had lost two Bf 109s, with a pilot killed. Six more *Gustavs* had been damaged.

The first mission for the 'Pumas' en masse came on 30 May, although due to 101/1 FS's losses on the 24th, the group could muster only 32 aircraft. Maj Heppes led the formation aloft, which consisted of Group Staff with four fighters, 101/1 and 101/2 FSs with eight apiece and 101/3 FS with 12. Taking off at 1043 hrs, the group assembled 14 minutes later at 2500 m over Veszprém. 'Rock Centre' then directed them to Alsólendva. Reaching Nagykanizsa at 1110 hrs, and cruising at 7000 m, the group duly changed course for Szombathely and arrived at its destination at

Ens Dezső Szentgyörgyi was not only the leading ace of the Hungarian Air Force, he was also its most highly decorated fighter pilot. By the end of the war he had claimed 32.5 kills *(Punka Archiv)*

The 'Pumas'' lair for much of 1944 – Veszprém airfield, north of Lake Balaton, in Hungary. 101 FG sortied from here during its numerous clashes with USAAF bomber formations, and their escorts *(Punka Archiv)*

1128 hrs. Information from fighter control, which was supplied by ground observation and German radar, was especially poor that day, and the Hungarians made no contact with the enemy. All 32 aircraft duly returned to Veszprém without firing a single shot.

The real test for the 'Pumas' came on the morning of 14 June when 32 aircraft were scrambled, under the command of Capt Horváth, to intercept some 600 bombers, and their escorts, which were attacking the nitrogen works at Pét and oil refineries near Budapest. The 8th *Jagddivision* also sortied 80 Bf 109s and Fw 190s from Austrian airfields.

The first USAAF aircraft encountered on this day were P-38 Lightnings caught strafing the airfield at Kecskemét, which was home to a squadron of Luftwaffe Me 323 transports. German and Hungarian fighters clashed with the P-38s within a triangular area between Lake Balaton and the Bakony and Vértes mountains, and there were fierce dogfights over Pétfürdő and Veszprém. Flak units downed 11 aircraft, German fighters claimed two and the Hungarians destroyed eight. German losses are not known, but Hungarian pilot Lt Gyula Király was killed and Lt Pál Forró made an emergency landing. Two more Bf 109s were damaged.

The Hungarian tactics employed on 14 June were as follows. Group Staff and 101/1 FS attempted to get close to the bombers, while 101/2 FS provided protection from the flanks and 101/3 FS flew top cover. Everything seemed to be going according to plan until 101/2 FS ran into a formation of P-38s of a similar strength. With the flank cover overwhelmed, pilots of 101/1 FS had to break off their attack on the bombers and engage the P-38s instead. A massive fighter battle developed, and during the course of the engagement five-kill P-38 ace 1Lt Louis Benne of the 49th FS/14th FG was attacked by four German fighters and shot down – but not before he had himself claimed two Bf 109 kills (in P-38J-15 42-104229) to take his final tally to five. Benne bailed out of his burning Lightning and was captured when he came down near Pétfürdő.

101/2 FS's Lt Forró, Cpl/Maj Szentgyörgyi and Sgt Fábián each shot down a P-38, as did 101/3 FS's Lts Béláváry, Molnár, Pávai-Vajna, Dániel and Debrödy. A further two P-38 confirmations were withdrawn, and two B-24s were recorded as probables.

Two days later the largest enemy formation to date flew over Hungary, with several bomb groups being intercepted over Lake Balaton as usual.

Cpl/Maj István Fábián (left) and Sgt Dezső Szentgyörgyi – two of 101/2 FS's most successful aces – share a joke in front of a Bf 109G-2/R6. Both men claimed a P-38 apiece during the 14 June 1944 clash between the 'Pumas' and 700+ USAAF fighters and bombers sent to attack oil refineries near Budapest. No fewer than eight Lightnings were claimed to have been destroyed by pilots from 101 FG on this day *(Punka Archiv)*

Seven P-38Js were downed by 101 FG on 16 June, including this 14th FG machine which belly-landed in in a field near Cegléd. It had been badly shot up by 101/3 FS's Lt Mihály Karátsonyi, who was making his combat debut on this day *(Garay via Punka)*

Against the USAAF's 658 bombers and 290 fighters, the 'Pumas' scrambled just 28 aircraft at 0904 hrs. Fighting broke out over the lake at between 6000 and 7000 m. 101/1 FS singled out a formation of Liberators, but within seconds the Hungarian unit had been scattered by escorting fighters. Dogfighting both individually and in pairs, the 'Pumas' took on P-38s and P-51s, and had claims for 16 kills confirmed upon returning to base. Three more P-38s were listed as probables, whilst a Lightning that went down following a mid-air collision was not awarded as a victory.

1/Lt Bejczy, Lts Debrődy and Karátsonyi and Sgts Mátyás and Kovács of 101/3 FS each claimed a P-38, while 101/2 FS's Cpl/Maj Lőrincz was credited with two P-38s and Lt Tóth a 'P-47' (later amended to a P-51). Allied losses were confirmed as four B-24s, seven P-38s and one P-51. Despite these successes, this engagement had been the toughest so far for the 'Pumas'. Five pilots were dead and two had been wounded, and six aircraft had been totally destroyed and seven damaged.

The greatest surprise for the Hungarians had been the two kills scored by Cpl/Maj Mátyás Lőrincz, who was flying his first ever combat mission. Wingman to Lt Kőhalmy, he claimed his two kills when four P-38s latched onto the tail of his leader's Messerschmitt. Kőhalmy was shot down before his wingman could intervene, and distraught at his loss, Lőrincz proceeded to despatch two P-38s – one of which collided with a third Lightning, and this also crashed. The latter kill was never officially confirmed, however. Lőrincz got a field promotion to sergeant.

The Hungarians also suffered losses on 16 June, this 101/3 FS Bf 109G-6 being one of 13 *Gustavs* either destroyed or damaged *(Punka Archiv)*

Lt Tóth shot down his opponent over Simontornya, although his brave battle against a numerically superior enemy ultimately proved to be futile when he was in turn forced to bail out after his machine was badly shot up. This was the fourth time he had jumped from a fighter in flight, having bailed out three times whilst serving on the Eastern Front. Once on the ground, Tóth met up with the P-51 pilot that he had just shot down! They chatted until the American was picked up by a Hungarian Army patrol!

Minutes after claiming his P-38 Lt Karátsonyi was also hit, forcing him to crash-land his Bf 109G-6. Both sides paid a high price in men and machinery on 16 June *(Punka Archiv)*

Lt Pávai-Vajna poses alongside the shattered remains of his Bf 109G-6 V.8+04. Another victim of the 16 June battle, he was just about to land at Veszprém in order to refuel and rearm when he was jumped by four P-38s. His engine in flames, Pávai-Vajna hastily belly landed and ran from the machine under fire. He was lucky to escape with a minor head wound *(Hemmert via Punka)*

Like Cpl/Maj Mátyás Lőrincz, Lt Mihály Karátsonyi of 101/3 FS had also enjoyed success on his first mission when a P-38 suddenly appeared in front of him. He opened fire, then tried to get away from a clutch of pursuing fighters by diving vertically down. Flying close to the tree-tops towards Veszprém, Karátsonyi heard a call for help from a pilot named Pászthy. He answered immediately but got no reply. Pászthy, who had been wounded seconds after making the call, had bailed out, but his parachute had caught on the tail of his Bf 109 and he was dragged down.

A 'Puma' emblem is applied to the nose of a newly-delivered Bf 109G-6. Due to the heavy losses of 14 and 16 June, come the 17th the 'Pumas' had only 22 combat-ready fighters available. However, ten days of inactivity in Hungarian airspace saved the group from total annihilation *(Karátsonyi via Punka)*

Meanwhile, Lt Pávai-Vajna was hurrying back to his airfield to refuel and rearm. Just as he was about to land, four Lightnings pounced on him. With a flaming engine, he bellied in and ran from the burning machine. The P-38s strafed both the Bf 109 and its pilot several times, but Pávai-Vajna escaped with only a head wound.

As for the American bombers, they did not attack any Hungarian targets that day!

Due to the heavy losses suffered by the 'Pumas' in June, the group

had only 22 combat-ready fighters available on 17 June. It seemed that Hungary's sole home defence fighter group would not be in action for much longer, but ten days of inactivity in local airspace saved it from being wiped out. Then, on the morning of the 26th, observers reported the approach of a large American formation – 677 bombers and 300 fighters of the Fifteenth Air Force were heading for western Hungary. The entire 'Puma' force of 30 fighters scrambled at 0830 hrs and headed for Győr, where a fierce battle took place between 7000 and 10,000 m.

The Hungarians were ordered to join German fighters that had intercepted 100 USAAF aircraft over Bratislava, but only 101/1 FS arrived in time to engage the enemy. At 0903 hrs, as the unit attacked a 90-strong formation, 101/1 FS's second flight spotted Lightnings carrying out a low-level attack on the road between Bodajk and Zirc, in the Bakony Mountains. Using their greater height, the Hungarians effected a textbook bounce, allowing flight commander 1/Lt Irányi to down a P-38J (43-28771), which hit the ground and burst into flames north of Tés.

In 20 minutes the 'Pumas' claimed five confirmed kills, and besides Irányi's success, group CO Maj Aladár Heppes was credited with two B-24s (giving him ace status), Sgt Lajos Buday got another Liberator (his first of ten kills) and Sgt Takács claimed a P-51B (43-6921). Three Hungarian fighter pilots were killed, however.

The following day 331 USAAF bombers, escorted by 100 fighters, attacked Budapest. The 'Pumas' were sent into action with 24 aircraft, the brunt of the fighting falling to 101/2 and 101/3 FSs. North of the city, three bombers and one fighter were shot down and confirmed without loss to the Hungarian units. Sgt/Maj Dezső Szentgyörgyi of 101/2 FS claimed the fighter (P-51B 42-106498), while fellow ace Lt Lajos Tóth downed a B-17. Finally, future 10.5-kill ace Lt József Málik of 101/3 FS was credited with his first full victories in the shape of a B-17 and a B-24.

On 30 June 450 bombers and 160 escort fighters were detected approaching Lake Balaton, heading for Budapest. All 101 FG fighters were scrambled at 0845 hrs to intercept them, as were 17 aircraft from the 8th *Jagddivision* – 12 Bf 110s and Me 410s and five Bf 109s.

The fighting commenced above Zalaegerszeg-Tapolca, and so fierce was the Axis resistance that one Allied formation of 27 heavy bombers turned back short of the target. The fighters separated six bombers from

A veteran of 65 combat missions, 1/Lt László Dániel finished the war with 8.5 kills, including two shared B-24s. His aircraft sported victory marking on the tail, a practice that was rare in the Royal Hungarian Air Force *(Vasváry via Tobak)*

Exhaust streaked from high altitude interceptions at full throttle, this otherwise clean Bf 109G-6 was photographed in a revetment at Tapolca airfield during the summer of 1944 *(Punka Archiv)*

the rest of the formation and shot down three B-24s, one of which exploded upon crashing in the mountains. The second went down south-east of Nemesvita, the bombing bursting into flames after its crew failed in their attempt to make an emergency landing between a road and a railway line. The third was hit over Szigliget and fell away on fire.

The rest of the bombers carried on north-west towards Germany, and a fourth B-24 fell to concentrated attacks by several Bf 109s. Lt Ernő Karnay of 101/1 FS, Sgt István Fábián (who was already an ace) of 101/2 FS and Ens András Huszár of 101/3 FS were each credited with a B-24 destroyed. Three other victories involving a B-24 and two P-38s were not confirmed. Several badly damaged Hungarian aircraft went down, with one pilot, Ens Gyula Zsiros, losing his life.

On 2 July American weather reconnaissance aircraft flew over Hungary from the direction of Barcs-Berzence, following the route the Fifteenth Air Force's bombers would normally take on their return leg to Italy. At 0900 hrs, when 712 bombers and 300 escort fighters crossed the Hungarian border and headed towards Lake Balaton, the 'Pumas' despatched just 18 fighters to intercept them. The Germans launched

Local people get a close-up look at a 30-plus mission veteran B-24D that was shot down in a bombing raid on Hatvan, south of Lake Balaton, in mid 1944. Details of who shot it down, or the final fate of its crew, remain unknown *(Fejes via Punka)*

Cpl/Maj Sándor Beregszászi stands in front of his aircraft at Ferihegy in early 1944. This specially posed propaganda photograph was taken soon after the 'Pumas' had fully re-equipped with Hungarian-built Bf 109Gs. Note the highlighted underwing cross *(Punka Archiv)*

Lt László Molnár is congratulated by fellow pilots and groundcrew at Veszprém after shooting down two B-24s on 7 July 1944. He would claim a further 2.5 Liberators before the month was out, taking his final tally to 25.5 kills *(Tobak via Punka)*

An official portrait of fourth-ranking Hungarian ace Lt László Molnár *(Punka Archiv)*

Me 410s from I./ZG 76, Bf 110s from the I./ZG 1 and Bf 109s from II./JG 27. The bombers' targets were refineries and airfields in Budapest, although poor aiming saw widespread damage inflicted on nearby residential areas. At Ferihegy, most of the aircraft on the airfield were either damaged or destroyed. A larger American formation attempted to bomb the refineries at Almásfüzito, but flattened two nearby villages instead.

The Mustang-equipped 4th FG of the Eighth Air Force also took part in this maximum effort raid, the group being involved in aerial battles stretching from Lake Balaton to Budapest. The Hungarians destroyed three B-24s, one B-17 and two P-51Bs, although the Mustang escorts got the upper hand over Pusztaszabolcs and downed solitary German and Hungarian fighters near Enying. Both pilots bailed out.

More losses were suffered over Balatonkenese, where three US fighters chased Cpl/Maj Sándor Beregszászi for several minutes before shooting him down. He failed to survive the crash. Lt Karnay and Cpl/Maj Takács were also lost at this time. To make matters worse, the surviving 'Puma' fighters were shot at over Budapest by friendly flak.

The daily communiqué listed the 'Puma' victories as follows – Maj Heppes, one B-24, 1/Lt Irányi of 101/1 FS, two B-24s (to make him an ace) and fellow squadron members 1/Lt Lajos Benkő, one B-24, Cpl/Maj Pál Szikora, a B-17 and a P-51, and Sgt Zoltán Raposa, one P-51. Among the pilots of 101/2 FS, Sgt/Maj Szentgyörgyi and Cpl/Maj Károly Faludi each got a B-24, while Ens Leó Krizsevszky shot down a P-51. In 101/3 FS, future ace Lt László Dániel was credited with a P-38 and leading ace Lt Debrődy got a Mustang for his 21st kill.

After the war it emerged that Krizsevszky, whose claim was not confirmed at the time, had downed the P-51B (43-6746) of 15-kill ace Lt Ralph 'Kid' Hofer. One of the Eighth Air Force's most successful fighter pilots at the time of his death, Hofer, of the 334th FS/4th FG, was found in the wreckage of his aircraft in the mountains of Yugoslavia, some 500 kms from where the fighting had taken place. Aside from his loss, the Allies confirmed that ten B-24s, three B-17s and six P-51s had been downed over Hungary.

The 'Pumas' did not have long to wait for the next raid, for on the morning of 7 July they received three alert warnings. This time some 560 USAAF bombers and 250 escort fighters were heading for Hungary. Ten 101 FG aircraft scrambled, and they had reached 3000 m when they attacked several P-38s. The first bounce was successful, for two fighters were downed, one crashing at Tét and the other near Pápa. The 'Pumas' then had to break off their attack when 20 more Lightnings appeared.

Climbing to the north, they soon spotted two groups of bombers, each consisting of 30 aircraft, at 3800 m. A few of them were straggling behind the main formation, so Maj Heppes, 1/Lt Irányi and Lts Benkő and Barsy went after a trio of visibly damaged Liberators. Heppes soon ran out of ammunition, leaving the others to press on with the attack. One bomber tried to escape back towards the south, but it was intercepted by Lt Barsy. Flak batteries then opened fire, hitting the bomber several more times. The crew duly bailed out of the burning aircraft, which hit the ground near Hajmáskér and exploded.

Lt Barsy then attacked a second bomber in the middle of the formation, and eight crewmen hastily bailed out of the smoking aircraft, which went down south of Hajmáskér and exploded in rocky terrain. Lt Benkő chased a Liberator flying on the right-hand side of the formation, but he had to break off his attack when flak burst erupted around him. Waiting until the bomber was over Lake Balaton, he made a frontal attack on the B-24, opening fire from just 500 m. By now two of the Liberator's four engines were on fire, so the crew started to jump clear. Moments later, some 1500 m above the lake, the bomber was torn apart by an explosion.

That same day Lt Tóth made a P-38 force-land near Tét, although he was in turn shot down by one of 12 Lightnings that arrived too late to save their comrade. Tóth leapt from his fighter close to the ground, his parachute opening at a height of just 100 m. Now an 'ace' with this bailing out, Tóth's P-38 kill took his score to 13 victories.

Fellow ace György Debrődy damaged a P-38 in the same engagement, after which he and his wingman attacked a bomber formation and brought down a B-17. Debrődy's Messerschmitt was then hit several times by enemy fighters, his oxygen cylinder exploding and peppering the Hungarian with splinters. He managed to land at Veszprém on just one wheel, although his aircraft was badly damaged.

Miraculously, the 'Pumas' had lost only Tóth's aircraft in combat, with Debrődy's Bf 109 all but written off. Against this, Maj Heppes had downed a B-24, as had Lt Benkő of 101/1 FS and Sgt Lőrincz of 101/2 FS. Cpl/Maj Faludi, also from 101/2 FS, had destroyed two P-38s, while Lt Tóth had claimed a third. 101/3 FS's Lt Gellért Barsy downed a B-24, while single B-17s had fallen to Lt Debrődy and Ens Huszár. Finally, Lt Molnár had boosted his tally to 20 kills with the destruction of two B-24s.

Between 9 and 13 July air activity was halted over Hungary due to bad weather. Conditions improved on the 14th, and that morning 450 bombers and 150 fighters attacked Budapest. 101 FG scrambled all three squadrons, but their total strength consisted of just 16 Bf 109s.

Five-kill ace Lt Mihály Karátsonyi was shot down and badly burned on 7 August 1944. However, he was back in action by December. Karátsonyi was awarded the Iron Cross, First and Second Class. *(Vasváry via Tobak)*

Lt László Molnár in his Bf 109G-6 V.8+48 in July 1944. He enjoyed great success in this machine during the course of the month *(Winkler via Punka)*

Lt Karátsonyi and three other pilots from 101/3 FS succeeded in surprising a squadron of P-38s, and the former soon shot one of them down. The falling aircraft collided with a second Lightning, and both fighters spiralled away, their pilots having to bail out. The appearance of more P-38s forced the Hungarians to flee, with Karátsonyi being chased almost all the way to Szolnok by several twin-boomed machines.

Two days later 380 bombers and 150 escort fighters passed over Transdanubia in three waves on their way to Vienna. The 'Pumas' scrambled 12 aircraft and claimed four bombers shot down. Lt Benkő of 101/1 FS destroyed a B-17, while a B-24 fell victim to Lt Gellért Barsy of 101/2 FS, and another Liberator was claimed by Sgt/Maj Szentgyörgyi

(taking his overall tally to 10.5 kills). The final B-24 fell to Bejczy of 101/3 FS.

Lt Benkő had attacked his B-17 over Austria, bringing it down near St Johann. He was duly awarded the Iron Cross, Second Class, by the Germans for this success, although his own air force failed to confirm his kill!

Relative calm was experienced over Hungary between 17 and 25 July. On the 26th, a small Hungarian force intercepted bombers heading for Austria, and in combat over the latter country Lt Molnár downed a B-24. However, its defensive fire claimed the life of Ens Leó Krizsevszky.

At 0830 hrs the following day, about 500 American aircraft penetrated Hungarian airspace from the south-west, making for Budapest. 101 FG scrambled all three squadrons, which in turn met up with aircraft from the 8th *Jagddivision* over Balatonfüred. Taking advantage of superior height, the Axis fighter force attacked a formation of 80 aircraft at an altitude of 7,000 m between Székesfehérvár and Tata. Following their first pass, the fighter pilots now picked out six damaged B-24s that had fallen behind the formation, and duly shot four of them down.

The Hungarians were about to start their second attack when the escorts intervened, forcing the 'Pumas' to break off and engage the fighters instead. In the ensuing dogfight the 101 FG pilots downed two P-51s without loss. The day ended with Lt Debrődy and Sgt/Maj Szentgyörgyi of 101/2 FS each having brought down a B-24, while squadronmate Lt Kovács claimed a P-51. 101/3 FS's Lt Mihály Karátsonyi and Lt Molnár each downed a B-24, while a Mustang fell to Cpl/Maj Zoltán Skulka.

The enemy raids continued, increasing the workload for the few remaining 'Pumas'. Early in the morning of 30 July, 300 aircraft attacked Budapest and the oil fields at Lispe. A Hungarian flight of four Bf 109s succeeded in downing two straggling B-24s over Nádasladány.

Cloudy weather then prevented aerial activity until 7 August when, against a backdrop of scattered cumulus, 357 heavy bombers and 117 escort fighters arrived over south-west Hungary in the early morning hours, bound for targets in Poland.

101 FG sortied once again, 18 fighters being assigned the job of covering German Bf 109G-6/R6 'heavy' fighters. In a one-sided dogfight with American Mustangs, the Hungarians lost eight aircraft and the Germans at least nine. In return, only two victories were claimed by Lt József Málik of 101/2 FS and Lt Mihály Karátsonyi of 101/3 FS. Having

This 20 mm cannon was stripped out of a battle-damaged Bf 109 and used by the Hungarians to defend one of its airfields from marauding USAAF fighters *(Kovács via Punka)*

just 'made ace', Karátsonyi was in turn forced to bail out of his blazing fighter with serious burns. In a black day for the 'Pumas', Ens János Nyemetz and leading ace Lt László Molnár lost their lives in combat.

Having claimed 25.5 kills (18 Soviet and 7.5 American), 23-year-old Molnár died on his 132nd combat mission. He was posthumously promoted to 1st lieutenant.

On 9 August Győr, Budapest and Almásfüzitő were attacked by bombers, and the intercepting 'Pumas' were not only fired on by the enemy, but also by friendly flak. Several days later the group received better armed Bf 109s, which the pilots hastily converted onto.

The 21st saw the Allies launch an air offensive against Hungarian airfields, with two squadrons of Me 210 fast bombers suffering heavy losses at Hajdúböszörmény. That same day bomber gunners scored hits on Cpl/Maj Zoltán Skulka's Bf 109, fatally wounding its pilot.

On the 22nd the USAAF attacked the airfield at Szombathely, where the Hungarian Elementary Flying Training School and German night-fighters were based. Axis fighters clashed with the enemy near Pápa, and over nearby Kiskomárom American fighters claimed the life of 5.5-kill ace Sgt Pál Kovács. At 1330 hrs Cpl/Maj Tibor Hoy's aircraft was also hit several times, although he made a successful forced landing under fire near Keszthely. Only two of the B-24s that the Hungarians claimed shot down that day were confirmed (credited to Sgt/Maj Szentgyörgyi and Cpl/Maj Lajos Buday), these victories bringing the 'Pumas' their 99th and 100th kills.

Although USAAF raids continued on a near daily basis, a shattered 101 FG was pulled out of action until the beginning of October. According to military records, the group had downed 104 American aircraft between May and August 1944 – 15 Mustangs, 33 Lightnings and 56 heavy bombers (Flying Fortresses and Liberators).

P-38J 42-104105 crash-landed near Sümeg on 22 August 1944. Note its prominent nose art, in contrast to anything displayed by the 'Pumas' *(Punka Archiv)*

Lt Pál Bélaváry (left) and Lt László Dániel pose for a photograph at Veszprém in mid 1944. Bélaváry was killed when his Bf 109 was bounced by P-51s whilst he was attempting to land at Veszprém on 12 October *(Dániel via Tobak)*

These figures suggest that claimed, but unconfirmed, victories were included in this tally because of the long time it took for confirmation to come through. During this time the group lost 18 pilots in combat, one during the 8 July bombing raid and one on a training flight.

By the end of August 1944, the 2nd Soviet Ukrainian Front, along with those Rumanian army units that had switched to the Soviet side, had forced the German South-Ukraine Army Group to pull back its troops into Hungary after abandoning the passes through the Eastern and Southern Carpathians. The move, first to the Tiszántúl, east of Hungary's River Tisza, and then to Transdanubia, was not an easy one for *Luftflotte* 4's approximately 500 aircraft and personnel. This so-called 'relocation' was really a retreat, which left Hungarian airfields packed full.

The Red Army soon reached Hungary's eastern and south-eastern borders. At the beginning of October 1944, both the 2nd and 3rd Ukrainian Fronts were supported from the air by some 2000 aircraft of the 5th and 17th Air Armies. Also committed to the campaign were the 1st and 4th Rumanian armies, with 113 aircraft of various types.

German and Hungarian aircraft patrol together in the late summer of 1944, 'White 6' being flown by Lt Pál Bélaváry. He was killed at the controls of W-0+52 when it was shot down on finals near Veszprém by P-51s *(Dániel via Tobak)*

Opposing them were *Luftflotte* 4 and approximately 800 aircraft of the Royal Hungarian Air Force.

In the middle of September 101 FG was expanded into a wing that consisted of two groups. 101/I FG, comprising 1, 2 and 3 FSs, was under the command of Capt Scholtz, while 101/II FG, controlling 4, 5 and 6 FSs, was led by Maj Gyula Csathó.

Between 1 September and 7 November the Hungarian fighter force engaged the USAAF on just five occasions. The clash on 12 October came about after the three squadrons of 101/I FG had attacked Soviet Air Force units supporting troops crossing the River Tisza, near Szeged. Returning home, the group was bounced by American P-51s south-east of Lake Balaton. The first Hungarian squadron had reached Veszprém airfield and was about to land when it was attacked by Mustangs. The pilots scattered, and Lt Kálmán Nánási, flying W-0+49, was forced to make an emergency landing among the reeds on the shore of Lake Balaton. Private 1st Class Erdész was shot down in W-0+88 at Pétfürdo, and Lt Béláváry was killed when his aircraft (W-0+52) crashed near the airfield. Lt Károly Balogh was also lost when he came down near Veszprém. Several other aircraft landed at other airfields.

Sgt Ambrus Dóra of 101/2 FS managed to escape from the Mustangs' hail of bullets by breaking sharply to the left and belly-landing his damaged Bf 109 in a meadow at Tótvázsony. The Mustangs then made several strafing runs on his burning aircraft, but Dóra was saved by his back armour plating. Meanwhile, two P-51Bs (43-24852 and 43-25881) were brought down by Sgt Lőrincz and Lt Málik.

That same day, the daily air force communiqué announced that two squadrons from 101 FW, and 5/1 NFS, were being placed under the command of the German 8th Home Defence Fighter Division.

From 13 October, American fighters systematically attacked Hungarian-German airfields in Transdanubia, shooting down, or damaging, many aircraft during transit flights or on the ground. For much of October Hungarian fighters were sent into combat solely against the Soviet Air Force and communist troops that were attacking across the Great Plain.

**Its Hungarian markings in full colour, Bf 109G 'Red 2' was the regular mount of 13-kill ace Lt László Pottyondy on the Soviet front during the autumn of 1944** (*Bernád Archiv*)

Cpl/Maj Mátyás Lörincz is seen at Veszprém in the summer of 1944 with the unit commander's dog. Shooting down two Lightnings (a third crashed when it was in collision with one of those shot down) on his combat debut on 16 June earned him field promotion to the rank of sergeant. His score stood at six when he was killed in action on 5 November *(Punka Archiv)*

102/2 FS's Ens István Kálmán had scored 12 kills by war's end, all of which were claimed against Soviet opposition between September 1944 and March 1945 *(Tobak via Punka)*

In October, 1 and 2 FSs of 102 FG returned to home soil after fighting on the Soviet Front. Now the group would be fighting the communists from Hungarian airfields instead.

On 1 November its pilots were in action again, fighting alongside aircraft from 101 FW. The Hungarians intercepted Boston bombers, and their escort fighters, attacking German-Hungarian troops near Cegléd. Future aces Ens István Kálmán, from 102/1 FS, and 1/Lt Ferenc Málnássy, from 102/2 FS, each shot down a Boston, while newly crowned ace Capt László Pottyondy, also from 102/2 FS, downed an La-5. The following day the Hungarians were again fighting over Cegléd, and this time 102/4 FS's 1/Lt György Bánlaky and Sgt Lajos Molnár shot down an Il-2 and an La-5 respectively south-east of the city. Lt László Frankó was listed as missing, however.

Despite 102 FG carrying out low-level attacks against Soviet troops throughout the day, the enemy's rapid advance eventually caused 102 FS to move from Ferihegy to Budaőrs, west of the Danube, on 2 November.

The following day 101/4 FS enjoyed more successes when 1/Lt Béla Füleki and Ens Mihály Sziráki each downed an Il-2 near Tiszasqly.

On the 4th a flight from 101/3 FS was sent to patrol over Szolnok. Led by squadron leader 1/Lt József Bejczy, the four Bf 109s took off at 0900 hrs. The weather soon deteriorated, and no enemy aircraft were encountered. Attempting to get below a layer of thin cloud, the pilots spotted a series of long parallel tracks in a field which had been made by Russian tanks trying to conceal themselves in the numerous haystacks that covered the

Lt József Bejczy, seen here in Hungary in 1943, flew more than 100 combat missions on the Eastern Front from 1942 onwards. Claiming four kills in the east, he destroyed a P-38 and a B-24 in 1944 to 'make ace'. As previously mentioned, he was lost whilst attempting to strafe Red Army tanks near Szolnok, in Hungary, on 4 November 1944 *(Punka Archiv)*

farmland. It was at this point that veteran pilot Bejczy (he was 28) made a fatal mistake. Turning back towards the field, he lost height to commence a strafing run, thus indicating to the Russians that they had been spotted. All hell broke loose as the tanks filled the sky with machine gun fire. There was a blinding flash and Bejczy was hit, his aircraft going down in a shallow dive and exploding when it struck the ground south of Abony. 1/Lt Debrődy was promoted to take his place as CO of 101/3 FS.

On the afternoon of 5 November about 500 aircraft of the Fifteenth Air Force attacked targets in the Vienna-Florisdorf area. Three squadrons from 101/I FG and a single unit from 101/II FG took off to intercept the raiders, teaming up with German aircraft once aloft. The Hungarians attacked the bomber formation near Tapolca, 101/3 'Drötkefe' FS flying top cover towards the rear, while ahead, and some 500 m below, 101/1 'Zongora' FS and, lower still, 101/2 'Retek' FS took on the 'heavies'.

The resulting engagement saw Lt György Michna of 101/1 FS, Lts József Málik (his fifth kill) and Lajos Tóth and Cpl/Maj Lajos Buday, all from 101/2 FS, each down a B-24. Two B-17 claims were not confirmed

1/Lt Ferenc Málnássy (right) chats with an unknown pilot at Budaörs in November 1944. Another pilot to enjoy considerable success against the Soviets in the final months of the war, he claimed 11 kills between October 1944 and March 1945 *(Tobak via Punka)*

A trio of aces between missions at Veszprém. They are, from left to right, Sgt János Mátyás (4.5 kills) and Lts György Debrődy (26 kills) and László Molnár (25.5 kills) *(Karátsonyi via Punka)*

61

because of incomplete documentation, although Sgt Pál Domján's victory over a P-51 was credited to him. Four Hungarian pilots died in the combat, including Sgt Mátyás Lőrincz, the Lightning marksman of the summer of 1944.

The Americans returned again on 6 November, and all four squadrons assigned to 101 FW scrambled their brand new Bf 109G-14s. Led by 1/Lt Debrődy, the units rendezvoused over Adony, where the pilots were ordered to head to the River Rába to provide cover for German heavy fighters. Far below, elements of the Hungarian force spotted four P-38s, which shook off their attackers after a short, but inconclusive, skirmish.

The following day marked the last organised mission by the 'Pumas' against the USAAF, when the two sides clashed near Tihany. Lt Michna was hit over Litér but managed to belly-land his damaged aircraft, whilst Lt Málik was forced to bail out.

101 FW's activities against the USAAF's Fifteenth Air Force ended on 7 November, and from then on its aircraft were kept busy fighting units of the Soviet 2nd and 3rd Ukrainian Fronts. Troops of the 2nd Ukrainian Front were nearing Budapest, and forces of the 3rd were crossing the Danube south of Mohács.

Despite the dreadful situation facing the Hungarian forces, 101 FW's aircraft losses were still being made good, and older model Bf 109Gs upgraded and re-equipped with a methanol/water boost system. The latter saved Lt László Dániel, technical officer of 101/3 FS (and an 8.5-kill ace), on 5 November when he was chased by a Mustang for more than 30 minutes. Although the radiator of his Messerschmitt had been hit, he was able to get away and land safely at Tapolca.

More brand new replacement fighters (coded W-1+32, W-1+35, W-1+37, W-1+38 and W-1+42) arrived in early November, and on the 11th

1/Lt László Dániel is seen with his Bf 109G-6 at Veszprém during the summer of 1944. Despite continuing losses, surviving war-weary *Gustavs* were steadily re-equipped with a methanol/water boost system during the course of 1944, and Lt Dániel, technical officer of 101/3 FS, had one of these to thank for his life when, on 5 November, he was chased by a Mustang for more than 30 minutes. Although the radiator of his Messerschmitt had been holed, he was able to pull away from his foe and land safely at Tapolca *(Dániel via Winkler)*

Lt György Debrődy poses in his formal uniform in the summer of 1944. His long combat career finally came to an end on 16 November when, after shooting down an La-5 and a Yak-9 near Hatvan, Debrődy was hit in the stomach by the latter fighter and forced to make a crash-landing. Gravely wounded, his life was saved by emergency surgery. Debrődy was still recovering when the war ended *(Punka Archiv)*

Although only the third-ranking Hungarian ace with 26 kills, Lt Lajos Tóth was the second most highly decorated! Awarded the Iron Cross, Second and First Class, he completed 158 combat missions. Imprisoned by the communists post-war, Tóth was executed on 11 June 1951 *(Punka Archiv)*

101/I FG received nine more brand new aircraft – the required five-hour acceptance flights for these machines started immediately. That same day 102/1 FS was sent into action over Kecskemét, and two Il-2s were shot down by future 5-kill ace Lt Kálmán Szeverényi and Lt Csaba Szőts.

101 and 102 FGs flew another joint mission on the 13th, and duly became involved in a late afternoon combat over the Great Plain. 101/2 FS's Ens Szentgyörgyi downed a Yak-9 north of Jászkisér, fellow ace Sgt Fábián got a second north of Tápiószele and Cpl/Maj L Krascsenics and Lt Tóth added a third and fourth to the south. 102/2 FS's Lt Kálmán Szeverényi downed an Il-2 over Jászberény, while 1/Lt Ferenc Málnássy got his *Stormovik* over Jászapáti. Both pilots would later become aces.

By this time 102 FG Command had been established, and brought up to full strength. Maj József Kovács was put in command, with Capt Endre Nemes leading 102/1 FS and Capt László Pottyondy heading 102/2 FS.

On 16 November a smaller four aircraft formation from 101/1 and 101/3 FSs flew a fighter sweep over Jászberény, where the Hungarians ran into Soviet La-5s at 6000 m. One of the Bf 109G-14 pairs immediately made a frontal attack on the enemy aircraft, and Lt Debrődy hit an La-5 with cannon fire. The Lavochkin went down in flames. A second pair of *Gustavs*, led by Lt Tibor Tobak, then opened fire as their quarry turned away. Presenting Tobak's wingman with a perfect target, the La-5 was duly despatched by Lt Gyula Pintér.

The quartet carried on towards Hatvan, where they were attacked by several formations of Yak-9s. The Hungarians quickly climbed, and were soon embroiled in a series of dogfights over Nagykáta. Within a matter of minutes Debrődy spotted a Soviet pilot heading towards him, so he opened fire. The Yak-9 exploded in a ball of flames, although not before György Debrődy was himself hit in the stomach. Despite the severity of his wound, the 24.5-kill ace managed to force-land near Hatvan. Debrődy's life was saved by emergency surgery, although he never flew in combat again. 1/Lt Sándor Halasi was duly transferred from 101/1 to 101/3 FS to assume command of the wounded Debrődy's squadron.

Aside from 1/Lt Debrődy's La-5 and Yak-9 victories, Lts Pintér and Tobak and Cpl László Boldizsár each destroyed an La-5.

101/2 FS also saw considerable activity during mid November, having been sent into action in the most southern sector of the front. On the 16th, in a scrap with heavily armoured Il-2 ground-attack aircraft, Ens Szentgyörgyi (14.5 kills) and Lt Tóth (16 kills) boosted their scores when they each destroyed a *Stormovik*.

102 FG enjoyed more success on 17 November, when its pilots participated in a joint operation with Bf 109s from JG 52. Engaging Soviet bombers and ground-attack aircraft that were harassing Axis troops in the foothills of the Mátra Mountains, 102/2 FS CO Capt Pottyondy had a famous wingman on this mission – none other than the world's most successful fighter pilot, Hauptmann Erich Hartmann. During the course of the sortie both aces downed a Boston, Pottyondy's victim crashing near Ócsa and Hartmann's falling close to Erzsébetfalva.

Other kills were claimed on this day by 1/Lt Ervin Flóznik of 102/1 FS, who downed two Il-2s, while Cpl/Maj Buday (drafted in from 101/2 FS for this mission) shot down a Boston. On the 18th, at a joint German-Hungarian meeting at *Luftflotte* 4 headquarters, a decision was made to

Leading German ace (with 352 kills) Hauptmann Erich Hartmann (left), *Staffelkapitän* of 4./JG 52, poses with 13-kill ace Capt László Pottyondy in front of an aircraft from 102 FG. Sharing the airfield at Budaörs in November 1944, II./JG 52 and 102 FG regularly flew joint missions against the advancing Soviet forces. Indeed, on 17 November Erich Hartmann was flying as Pottyondy's wingman when each of them downed Bostons that were attacking targets around Budapest *(Barbas Coll)*

strengthen 101 FW by adding a third group (101/III) consisting of three squadrons.

Cloud and mist kept the Hungarians on the ground until late November, when one of 102 FG's squadrons moved from Budaörs to Inota, while the group itself was placed under the command of the 8th *Jagddivision*.

By early December the Soviet advance had progressed as far as the southern shores of Lake Balaton. 101/I FG was told to prepare to evacuate. On the 4th, three of the group's squadrons carried out low-level attacks against advancing Russian troops, as well as their supply lines between Siófok and Kaposvár. The following day the group was given the job of escorting German dive-bombers to Ercsi, where they attacked Russian troops crossing the river. 102/2 FS, meanwhile, covered aircraft from *Schlachtgeschwader* 2, which set about bombing and strafing Russian troops near Hatvan as they unloaded supplies and equipment from railway wagons. Soviet ground-attack and fighter aircraft took to the air to protect their comrades, but the Hungarian escorts managed to score several victories. 102/2 FS's Lt Málnássy 'made ace' by downing an Il-2 and an La-5, while Lt Miklós Nemere shot down a Yak-9. Ens István Kálmán and Lt Tóth, who were on loan from 102/1 and 101/2 FSs respectively, also shot down a Yak-9 apiece. Kálmán's success took his tally to five kills.

Despite 8 December being overcast, the Hungarian fighters flew several missions in response to the Red Army crossing the Danube and steadily advancing the frontline until it stretched between Lake Velencei and Budapest. Numerous air battles took place, and kills were made by the pilots of 101 FG's Wing Staff, as well as 101/1 and 101/2 FSs.

The pilots of 101/3 FS were tasked with providing fighter cover for German tank concentrations, as well as escorting Hungarian Me 210s on

bombing missions. Victorious pilots on this day were 101/I FG Staff's Ens Lajos Buzogány, who destroyed a Yak-9, 101/1 FS's Lt Michna, who also claimed a Yak-9 as well as an La-5, and Ens Szentgyörgyi of 101/2 FS, who downed a third Yak-9.

With the weather remaining foggy and misty, over the next few days the pilots switched between flying fighter sorties and escort missions. Two more kills were added to the list when Lt Tóth shot down a Yak-9 at Györköny and 1/Lt Gábor Szecsey got an Il-2 between Ajka and Kislöd.

On the 14th, 102/1 FS was sent into action against Il-2s of the Soviet 189th Ground-Attack Division and La-5s of the 288th Fighter Division in an effort to counter a Red Army attack on German forces, which were grouping for Operation *Spatlese*. Amid air combats which developed in the area between Veszprém, Balatonkenese, Balatonfőkajár and Balatonaliga, Lt György Horváth shot down an La-5, Ens István Kálmán two Il-2s and 1/Lt Ferenc Málnássy a third *Stormovik*. In a second sortie against supply lines around Hatvan, Málnássy downed two more Il-2s. On the return flight Cpl/Maj László Vargha went missing over Vác.

The Soviet Army's attack on Budapest commenced on 10 December from the direction of Lake Velencei in the south, the communists attempting to surround the Hungarian capital.

On 17 December Sgt Zoltán Nemeslaky and 1/Lt Béla Füleki of 101/4 FS scrambled to intercept a lone, damaged Liberator. After making several firing passes, the Hungarians watched as the bomber's crew started to bail out. The B-24 finally crashed south-west of Dunaföldvár.

New fighters arrived for 101 and 102 FG the following day, allowing the older *Gustavs* still equipped with 20 mm cannon to be passed on to 101/6 Fighter Training Squadron.

A suitably marked 102 FG machine sits at Budaörs airfield during November 1944, its pilot holding one of the many dogs that seemed to be an essential part of fighter units the world over! At the time, 102 FG was heavily involved in flying missions against Soviet aircraft targeting Budapest *(Petrick via Punka)*

On the 20th, both groups had enjoyed more success, with Ens Szent-györgyi of 101/2 FS claiming an Il-2 at Meggyespuszta, 1/Lt Géza Lója of 101/4 FS downing an La-5 at Ercsi-Kápolnásnyék and 1/Lt László Máthé of 102/1 FS destroying a second La-5 20 km west of Mezőtúr.

As the communists gained more territory, so the fighter pilots' workload increased. Aside from performing patrols and reconnaissance flights, the groups also had to escort bomber formations and provide close-support cover for troops on the ground. Time and time again requests would come through from the front asking for protection against Il-2s.

## TACTICS

Pilots who were facing Soviet aircraft for the first time were helped to find the enemy's weak points by those who had fought the communists since 1943. In respect to the ubiquitous Il-2, the main problems it posed for its Hungarian foes centred around its heavy armour and rear gunner. However, the tactics the Hungarians used against them were simple.

The fighters would fly to their assigned airspace and patrol at a height of 6000 m. Soviet fighters rarely flew at this height, as their job was to protect low-flying Il-2s. Instead, they ranged along the frontlines at heights of between 3000 and 4000 m. The Hungarians, making full use of their superior altitude, would break through the protective ring of fighters in a dive and fire a burst into the square radiator of the Il-2 from below and behind, usually at an angle of between 20 and 30 degrees. Regrouping for a second attack often guaranteed a dogfight with the *Stormoviks'* escorts.

The Hungarians did not use the Germans' so-called 'Katschmarek' tactic. This was where the flight leaders from each pair of fighters would circle at between 5000 and 6000 m, while their 'Katschmareks' (wingmen) would fly at the same height as the enemy and pass onto their leaders information about their foes' strength, height and direction.

The leader of each pair would then dive down fast, attack usually the aircraft at the rear, then pull out. As they climbed back up to their previous altitude, they would shoot down the second last Il-2 from below. The German pilots would have the advantage of speed during the attack, so by the time the escorts spotted them, it would be too late – they would already be regrouping for a new attack. The Germans considered Hungarian tactics, which inevitably involved dogfights, as brave but suicidal.

Observing any aircraft being shot down during a fast-moving dogfight was difficult, and confirmation of victories always took quite a long time. Therefore, it was not always possible to evaluate the effectiveness of the tactics that had led to the kill.

The flyers' tasks became more difficult because of cloudy, misty weather, which allowed the enemy to slip away more easily. For the Hungarians, flying under low cloud was dangerous because of Soviet flak. Flying above it was just as risky, for the fighters would be silhouetted against the clouds, thus providing an excellent target for enemy aircraft above them. There was the numerical superiority of the Soviets to deal with too.

The weather had cleared a bit by the afternoon of 21 December, allowing 101/2 FS to go into action near Lake Velencei, where its pilots came face-to-face with Soviet fighters. Three La-5s and Yak-9s were shot down, and one Hungarian aircraft was hit, its pilot suffering minor wounds. Meanwhile, the pilots of 101/3 FS were sent up to escort German

He 111s over Mór as they prepared to attack Soviet troops crossing the Danube near Érd. The Hungarians spotted a formation of Lavochkins early enough to get in between the He 111s and the La-5s. The Russians obviously got the message, for despite being greater in number, they broke off their attack and disappeared eastwards. During the day's operations Sgt István Fábián of 101/2 shot down an La-5, as did Cpl/Maj Lajos Krascsenics. Lt László Máthé of 102/1 claimed a Yak-9.

The Hungarians rated the La-5 and La-7 as the most dangerous Soviet fighters, while the Yak-3 and Yak-9 were only real rivals in the hands of experienced 'Guards' pilots.

With a shortage of pilots now beginning to manifest itself in Hungary, those individuals who had been ferrying aircraft in Germany were sent to frontline units, where they were paired with veteran combat pilots to gain fighting experience.

On 22 December violent air engagements took place between Hungarian and Russian formations between Veszprém and Budapest, the duels fought over the capital stretching almost as far as the Mátra mountains. In the day's first encounter, Capt László Pottyondy chased an Il-2 and finally shot it down over Csány. At 1235 hrs 101/3 FS was ordered to intercept a formation of *Stormoviks* that boasted heavy fighter protection near Várpalota. Two pairs of fighters were scrambled – Lt Tibor Tobak and Cpl/Maj Boldizsár, and Lt Sándor Halasi and Lt Rezső Fuszek. Staying below 1000 m due to low multi-layered cloud, Lt Tobak duly shot down a Yak-9 and an Il-2 near Székesfehérvár.

The Soviets had encircled Budapest by 24 December, and in the fighting that took place over the next month-and-a-half, it was the crews of the transport aircraft who had the most important, and difficult, job to do.

That day 4 and 5 FSs of 101/II FG downed single La-5s over Esztergom. Although 101/3 FS scored no victories, its pilots had successfully escorted German dive-bombers sent to attack Russian armour north-west of Székesfehérvár.

Records state that between 1 and 23 December, 101/I FG took part in 55 missions, flying 229 sorties. The unit downed 11 aircraft, and lost an identical number of Bf 109s. One pilot died and two were wounded. 101/II FG flew 26 missions during the same period, scoring five kills. Two pilots were wounded. Finally, 102 FG downed 11 aircraft, although its losses are not known. One pilot was listed as missing in action, however.

There was no let-up even on Christmas Day, with fighters escorting several bombers over the Vértes Mountains and the Danube Bend. Over Vértesacsa, 102/2 FS's Géza Szenteleky downed an Il-2 which was protecting Soviet forces that had encircled the capital. 1/Lt Halasi also destroyed a Rumanian IAR-38 near Bicske, but had to belly-land back at base when the right gear leg of 'W-1+25' would not lower.

By this time advancing Soviet troops were only 20 kms from Veszprém airfield. No missions were flown between the 26th and 31st due to fog, but preparations to evacuate the base went ahead nonetheless. On 30 December the crews that were to form 9 FS (101/III FG) flew into Kenyeri airfield, north-west of Veszprém, with brand new aircraft from Wiener Neustadt. At the same time, two squadrons formerly attached to 102 FG were placed under the command of 101 FW.

# THE LAST BATTLES

On 2 January 1945 Hungarian and German forces jointly launched Operation *Konrad I*, which was the first attempt made by Axis forces to liberate the beleaguered city of Budapest. Troops pushed forward towards Bicske in clear and sunny weather, while fighters headed for the skies over Budapest itself, as well as the Danube Bend, on vital reconnaissance missions. Air combat ensued over both locations. At Esztergom, future 9-kill ace Lt Kálmán Nánási reported shooting down two Il-2s, while Ens Tibor Murányi claimed a Yak-9. Returning from a fighter sortie over Budapest, Cpl/Maj Pozsonyi's W-0+99 of 101/3 FS spun on landing and was wrecked. It was a busy day for the Soviet Air Force too, with the 17th Air Army carrying out 671 sorties against German tanks pushing towards Budapest.

The next day strong winds blew over Transdanubia. Yet in spite of these tricky flying conditions, 101/I and 101/II FGs, as well as 102 FG, were sent into action on several occasions against aircraft of the Soviet 189th Ground-Attack and 288th Fighter Divisions, which were targeting German troops in the Küngös-Sárpilis area. Air battles were fought over the Vértes Mountains, east and south of Budapest, and over the encircled city itself, as Soviet troops advanced westward. The 5th Close-Support Army Air Corps flew 300 sorties that day north of Budapest.

101/I FG's 1 and 2 FSs claimed four victories, 101/1 FS's Cpl/Maj Pál Szikora downing a Yak-9 north-east of Fót and another at Ráckeresztúr. Fellow squadron member Lajos Buday 'made ace' when he destroyed an La-5 at Pázmánd, and 101/2 FS's Lt József Málik took his tally to 6.5 kills when he claimed a Yak-9 north of Gödöllő.

Group losses on the day were only partly due to the Soviets, for the real enemy on the 3rd was the wind. A number of Bf 109s were lost in take-off accidents when they either veered into each other or off the runway completely. Indeed, the losses suffered were so bad that 101/I FG was left with just one serviceable aircraft! 101/II FG, fighting in the southern sector, was luckier, with 101/4 FS's Lt Géza Lója downing a Yak-9 near Bajna. 101/5 FS also enjoyed success, with Lt Pál Balogh claiming an La-5 and Lt János Báthy, Lt Nánási and Cpl/Maj Nagy each destroying a Yak-9 over Bicske.

On 4 January, again over Bicske, it was the turn of Ens Szentgyörgyi to add to his growing score when, in W-1+77, he downed a well flown La-5. Lt Tóth also destroyed an La-5. Later, Lt József Szabó from 101/4 FS reported shooting down a Lavochkin fighter as well.

On the 6th the 'Pumas' were placed under the direct command of *Stab./JG 76*, which was in turn part of the 1st *Fliegerkorps*. The latter organisation controlled all German fighter units operating in this sector of the front. That same day, due to dense fog, the only flying was performed in the afternoon, and most of that was by the Germans. However, two pilots from 101/I FG that were performing a reconnaissance mission succeeded in shooting down an La-5 in a short encounter south-east of Székesfehérvár.

**Lt Kálmán Nánási of 101/5 FS flew his first combat mission on 27 June 1944, and enjoyed great success against the Soviet Air Force between December 1944 and March 1945. Having claimed nine victories, Nánási was himself killed by Soviet flak whilst strafing Red Army positions on 4 April 1945** *(Vasváry via Tobak)*

**Sgt Lajos Buday looks pleased with himself after claiming his seventh kill (a Yak-9) on 19 January 1945. Two months later, on 16 March, he was shot down and killed during an engagement with La-7s** *(Punka Archiv)*

The following day the fog turned to snow, and all aircraft were grounded. However, in a second attempt to liberate Budapest, Operation *Konrad II* was launched from Zámoly.

The 8th brought two more aerial victories when Lt Dániel and Ens Szentgyörgyi each shot down an La-5 north-east of Székesfehérvár. Over the next two nights more snow fell, and during the day fog blanketed the area. The airfields were shut.

But the ground war continued. The battle for Budapest became more and more intense, and the last emergency airfield within the city eventually fell to the Russians. When the weather allowed, the fighters were up again, with the fiercest fighting during *Konrad II* taking place over Zámoly. On the 11th a four-strong flight from 101/I FG was sent into action in the area, and it clashed with 20 Yak-9s. Ens András Huszár shot down a fighter but lost his wingman, Cpl/Maj Károly Erdész (flying W-1+82), in the process. Details of what happened to him emerged after the war. Erdész, having got lost, ran out of fuel and made an emergency landing behind Soviet lines. Huszár's victory could not be confirmed because he had no witnesses.

On the 11th 101/II FG was issued with new 30 mm cannon-armed aircraft, and in turn handed over its old 20 mm cannon-equipped machines to 101/6 Fighter Training Squadron. Within 72 hours the group had fitted MW 50 methanol/water boost systems to its new *Gustavs*.

The 12th brought an unsuccessful conclusion to *Konrad II*, which had been hampered by a lack of air support due to persistent dense fog.

Forty-eight hours later 101/I and 102 FGs got involved in a fight over Csepel Island, shooting down six aircraft. The victors were Lt János Kovács with one La-7 over Budapest, 1/Lt Málnássy with a Boston over Csepel and two La-5s over Baracska, Capt László Pottyondy with a Boston over Pilisvörösvár and Ens Béla Sörő with an La-5 over Ercsi. At the time 101/3 FS was covering armoured units and escorting bombers.

On the 15th 101/III FG began a compete reorganisation. Its core units were now ex-102 FG's 102/1 and 2 FSs, and veteran pilot Maj Kovács was put in charge. To bring the group up to full strength, many pilots were transferred in from training units. 1/Lt László Máthé was given command of 101/7 (formerly 102/1) FS, while Capt Pottyondy took control of 101/8 (formerly 102/2) FS.

The pilots of 101/III FG's 101/9 (formerly 102/3) FS, under the command of Capt István Békássy, had been in Germany during the second half of 1944 ferrying brand new Bf 109s and Fw 190s from the factories to the frontlines. Several of its pilots had also been involved in the Ardennes offensive. With the formation of this third group, 101 FW at last reached its full strength.

The weather in Hungary had marginally improved by 16 January when, under a damp and cloudy sky, two squadrons from 101/I FG provided bomber escort for Hungarian Me 210s sent to destroy a bridge over the Danube at Dunaföldvár. Despite thick fog, the operation had to go ahead to try to disrupt the enemy's supply lines. The raid was a success, and the fighters left the bombers and headed for home. It was then that the Hungarians noticed two Ju 52/3ms being attacked by four La-5s. 101/2 FS's Cpl/Maj Krascsenics attempted to get into a position to fire, but the Russians sensed the danger and broke off the attack, leaving the

101/3 FS's Cpl/Maj Károly Erdész went missing on 11 January 1945 in W-1+82 after his four-strong flight clashed with 20 Yak-9s over Budapest. Details of what happened to him emerged after the war. Erdész, having been separated from his flight leader during the dogfight, became lost and ran out of fuel. He was then forced to make an emergency landing behind enemy lines, resulting in his capture *(Tobak via Punka)*

Sgt István Fábián of 101/2 FS scored 16.5 confirmed and six unconfirmed victories between June 1943 and March 1945. A highly respected wingman, he was one of the first Hungarian pilots to receive the Iron Cross, First Class *(Punka Archiv)*

Sgt Lajos Krascsenics ended the war with four confirmed victories over Soviet fighters and one unconfirmed B-24 kill *(Krascsenics via Punka)*

Hungarians to chase them. Krascsenics eventually downed his La-5 south-west of Sárbogárd, while Sgt/Maj Fábián destroyed a second La-5 a few minutes later. He had earlier claimed a Pe-2 north of Pincehely and a Yak-9 over Sárszentmihály. Finally, squadronmate Ens Bartos downed an La-5 west of Sárdosd.

101/1 FS ace Ens L Buday also enjoyed success on the 16th, destroying a Yak-9 over Seregélyes, as did Lt Lajos Szőts of 101/3 FS.

On 18 January the 6th German Army tried again to break through to Budapest by launching Operation *Konrad III* from Várpalota-Balaton-akarattya. The Soviet 17th Air Army tried its level best to keep the Axis forces at bay, in spite of the bad weather and the absence of some of its units, which were pulling back to airfields on the eastern side of the Danube. The first day of the new offensive saw it carry out 718 sorties against tanks, troop concentrations and airfields, Soviet pilots duly claiming to have shot down 37 German and Hungarian aircraft.

The poor weather did not hamper the Hungarians of 101 FW either, the wing clashing over the main battlefield with Soviet bomber and fighter formations. 1/Lts Füleki and Lója and Ens Murányi were the first to see action when they spotted a lone Boston. Closing on it, bursts from the Hungarian leader's machine guns silenced the rear gunner's protective fire. Füleki then made the next pass, followed by Lója. He opened fire from close range and the bomber hit the ground.

Part of another formation, Cpl/Maj Krascsenics and Ens Bartos were horrified when they flew for several kilometres along a road near Bala-tonaliga that was littered with dead Axis soldiers and horses, as well as still smoking motor vehicles. They had been attacked by Il-2s. Keen to avenge their loss, the Hungarians headed for Székesfehérvár and duly caught up with several *Stormoviks* just a few minutes later as they headed south.

Bartos, enraged by what he had just seen, and forgetting he was flying as wingman, attacked one of them. Ignoring the rear-gunner's fire, he swung under it, blasting away at its radiator. The Il-2 went into a steep dive and crashed into a hillside. Krascsenics joined the attack, and soon a second Russian went down, giving its victor ace status. 101/1 FS's Ens Szentgyörgyi also destroyed an Il-2, as well as an La-5, close by.

More paired fighter sorties took place on the afternoon of the 19th, fog having ruled out any flying in the morning. Flying beneath a cloud base of just 500 m, Lts Cserny and Michna and Sgt Buday each downed a Yak-9 north-west of Tolna while patrolling south of the main battlefield.

The following day the German offensive reached the Danube and Axis tanks started to roll northwards – by now some 50 km of territory had been re-captured. 101/I FG was sent into action to protect the advancing troops, and in clear skies it met Il-2s and La-5s. In a running battle along the Danube the Hungarian pilots scored four kills.

On 21 January pilots fighting over Budapest reported that the parliament building and the Royal Palace were on fire. During their return trip to base, Lts Forró and Tóth each shot down an Il-2 over Pusztaszabolcs, while Cpl/Maj Nagy destroyed a Yak-9.

More clashes took place over Budapest on the 22nd, fighters from 101/I FG fighting battles with Yak-9s but without result. The Hungarian pilots reported seeing blown-up bridges over the Danube between Buda and Pest and thick clouds of smoke swirling over the whole city.

101/III FG also went into action on this day when a formation of six fighters attacked Russian close-support aircraft not far from a former German airfield on the eastern bank of the Danube. On their way back to base, the Hungarians ran into another enemy formation, but had to break off because of low fuel. Three kills were attributed to Ens Kálmán of 101/7 FS, the ace downing two Il-2s and a U-2 near Bugyi. Squadronmate 1/Lt László Máthé downed a Yak-9 12 kms north of Bugyi, while just a kilometre further east Lt Csaba Szőts claimed a second U-2. Finally, an La-5 fell to 101/8 FS's Capt Pottyondy at Ercsi.

After a four-day battle, Soviet troops pulled out of Szákesfehérvár on 22 January. That night a storm washed away crossings over the Danube, forcing the Soviet command to redeploy part of the 5th Air Army of the 2nd Ukrainian Front to protect stranded troops near Szákesfehérvár. Aircraft of the 17th and 5th Air Armies flew 1034 sorties that day, and reported shooting down 36 enemy aircraft.

Communist resistance was stubborn, however, and it slowly bore fruit, for a continual series of German attacks resulted in almost 300 Axis tanks being knocked out.

The following day 101/I and 101/II FGs were sent to Budapest to target Russian aircraft trying to protect roads leading from the south, as well as troop concentrations in the area. Later, the Hungarians were instructed to provide cover for several bombers attacking targets in the Vértes Mountains.

In a fierce air combat fought out south of the capital, the Bf 109 pilots had to work hard for their victories. For once their opponents were not slow close-support machines, but fighters flown by experienced pilots. Nevertheless, Lt Lajos Tóth of 101/2 FS downed an La-5 at Ercsi and another at Lovasberény, while fellow ace Lt Málik brought down an La-5 west of Ullő. Among the pilots of 101/4 FS, 1/Lt Béla Füleki shot down a Yak-9 south-west of Budapest, and a second Yakovlev fighter fell victim to Ens Murányi in the same area.

The weather over the next few days brought a respite for the Hungarian fighter pilots, as heavy snow restricted flying to a mere handful of missions. Then, during the night of the 26th, *Konrad III* (the operation the Germans had so hoped would liberate the troops trapped in the Hungarian capital) ended in failure.

The snow during this period was so heavy that runways at airfields could only be kept open by shovelling throughout the night. Then, on the 30th, more kills were achieved when pilots from 101/I FG reported shooting down a Yak-9 and an La-5. These were credited to Cpl/Maj Nándor Pozsonyi and Ens Szentgyörgyi, the former's claim being backed up by his flight leader, 1/Lt Halasi.

After this brief period of activity the weather closed in again, with fog, mist, snow and sleet halting missions until early February.

101/I FG's published summary of its January activities recorded the following statistics. Its pilots flew 83 missions (344 take-offs) and scored 28 victories, for the loss of three pilots missing in action, three Bf 109s written off and 26 damaged. The report for 101/II FG mentioned 53 take-offs, 26 victories and two pilots lost. Finally, 101/III FG's records list 15 victories and the loss of one pilot. All kills and losses occurred during the 20 days when the weather was deemed suitable for flying.

In one of many accidents that befell the 'Pumas' at Veszprém in the final months of the war, these two *Gustavs* collided whilst attempting to take off in high winds. Astoundingly, the pilot of W-1+43 emerged from the crash with only minor injuries, despite his cockpit being destroyed by the propeller of V.8+72 *(Zsák via Sinka)*

The month of February brought no improvement in the weather, yet on the 1st 101/II FG was told to move to Vönöck. The following day the weather cleared enough for missions to resume, and during clashes over Ráckeresztúr another victory was added to the list by Lt Málik (who had assumed command of 101/1 FS in the middle of January). His victim was a Pe-2 light bomber, this example being only the second of its type to be shot down by the 'Pumas' over Hungary.

The 3rd saw the day's operations fall victim to fog yet again, but on the 4th the sun was shining. By then 101/I FG had received 23 Bf 109G-10/U4 fighters, with a further three being supplied to 101/II FG. Both units were up to full strength again.

The first pilot to clash with the enemy on the 4th was Lt Nánási, who engaged La-5s over Budapest and emerged with a confirmed kill – his seventh. Later that same day 101/3, 101/4 and 101/5 FSs fought a series of battles south of Lake Velencei when they intercepted a formation of Bostons. For once the Soviet bombers defended themselves well, and 101/4 FS's Sgt Lajos Molnár was killed when his fighter was hit several times – but not before he had downed a Boston. Thanks to the intervention of the Hungarian fighters, the Soviet bomber crews dropped their loads without aiming and turned for home.

However, before they could reach the safety of their base at Kecskemét, two of their number had been destroyed during a series of attacks launched by the pursuing 101 FG pilots, who had chased the Bostons across the Danube. Aside from Molnár's kill, Cpl/Maj László Kérges of 101/5 FS also downed a Boston east of Kunszentmiklós.

Following nine days of truly abysmal weather, conditions began to improve on the morning of 13 February. Although dawning misty, the

Standing in the snow in early 1945, five Hungarian fighter pilots are joined by two of their Luftwaffe counterparts at an awards ceremony. They are, from left to right, unknown, Hauptmann Helmut Lipfert of II./JG 52 (who survived the war as *Kommandeur* of I./JG 53, having claimed 203 kills during the course of 700+ missions), Lt Lajos Tóth, Lt József Málik, 1/Lt Béla Füleki, 1/Lt Sándor Halasi and Cpl István Fábián *(Tobak via Punka)*

weather had cleared sufficiently by the afternoon to allow 101 FG to attempt to intercept a formation of American bombers heading back from a raid on Vienna. Flying over western Hungary, the bombers also dropped ordnance on Sopron and the railway station at Celldömölk.

At 1245 hrs six aircraft from 101/7 FS took off to engage a lone Flying Fortress (B-17G 44-6546 of the 97th BG) which had been spotted over Szabadbattyán at a height of 2000 m. Both engines on the bomber's right wing were on fire, and it was obvious that the B-17 was trying to reach Soviet territory, where its crew could make an emergency landing. The first pair of Messerschmitts were just getting into position to attack when seven of the bomber's crew started to bail out. Lt Kálmán Szeverényi duly delivered the coup de grace (for his fifth kill), and after concentrated machine gun and cannon fire, the bomber slowly fell away and hit the ground three kilometres north-east of Dég. Nine members of the B-17's ten-man crew bailed out successfully.

By mid February 1945 fuel shortages were becoming so acute for Axis fighter units that an order was issued stating that drop tanks should be jettisoned only in the event of air combat, or an in-flight emergency.

On the 15th 101/III FG was combined temporarily with 101/I FG, yet in spite of the better weather few missions were flown. The codes applied to the Hungarian *Gustavs* were also changed at this time, one and two-digit numbers being used instead of the letter and number combination that had been the norm since 1942. Each squadron was also allocated its own colour for its numbers, although some aircraft retained their old codes through to war's end.

The 18th and 19th saw sorties flown over the River Ipoly. On the latter date, Lt Szebeni, in W-0+60, shot down an La-5 west of Ipolyszalka, while Sgt/Maj Fábián (of 101/2 FS) and Cpl/Maj Pál Fülöp (of 101/5 FS) each claimed two Lavochkins apiece west of Tardos and Ipolyság. The group's sole loss was Lt György Horváth (of 101/7 FS), whose fighter was seen to go down in a steep dive over Esztergom.

From 20 February the mission tempo increased once again, with the Hungarians mounting patrols while the Luftwaffe attacked crossing points over the Danube. During the course of the day all three groups completed no fewer than 11 missions, 101/I FG putting up 24 aircraft, 101/II FG 27 and 101/III FG 12. Almost all the Hungarians became embroiled with enemy aircraft. For example, eight pilots from 101/8 FS were patrolling between 1007 and 1105 hrs when they noticed camouflaged Il-2s, and escorting fighters, 500 m above Szendehely. The *Stormoviks* attempted to escape by flying ever closer to the ground, and thus blending in with the terrain, while their escorting Yak-9s engaged the Hungarians.

Not far from the village of Szendehely, formation commander Capt Pottyondy succeeded in getting in behind one of the fighters, and he duly shot the fighter down (its left wing was almost torn off) with just a few rounds from his devastating Rheinmetall Borsig MK 108 30 mm cannon. The Yak exploded when it hit the ground.

The 21st was also a hard day for 101 FW, its three fighter groups undertaking 69 sorties during the course of nine missions flown in support of Hungarian Fw 190 ground-attack aircraft. The latter were heading for Esztergom and Komárom, where they bombed various river crossings. 101/I FG encountered Yak-9s over the target area, but the Soviet pilots shied away from a fight. Eight machines (in two flights of four) from 101/II FG were also covering the Fw 190s, and they clashed with a Russian fighter formation made up of assorted types of aircraft over Esztergom at between 3500 and 3700 m. 101/4 FS's Ens Sziráki quickly shot down a Yak-9 15 kms north-east of Esztergom, while Sgt László Nagy destroyed an La-5.

On 22 February eight 101/III FG machines had just taken off when Lt Szeverényi, CO of 101/7 FS, radioed Capt Pottyondy, his counterpart in 8/101 FS, to tell him that he had spotted more than a dozen Yak-9s just miles away. Moments later one of the Yaks pulled up and fired at the Messerschmitts, and although the shot was taken from some distance away, several bullets hit Szeverényi's radiator. The coolant quickly drained out of his DB 605, and it soon began to overheat, leaving Szeverényi with little choice but to force-land his crippled fighter.

Spotting a meadow with a frozen lake behind it near Tatatóváros, the ace hit the ground with some speed, which was barely reduced as the Bf 109 skidded over the frozen ground, skipped over a dike and broke through the ice, before coming to a halt half submerged in the freezing lake. Hypothermic and half drowned when retrieved from his shattered fighter, Szeverényi was rushed to hospital, where he died with his wingman and mechanic sat by his bedside just hours later.

**Blanketed in snow, Veszprém airfield, in Hungary, was home to 101 FW until the last weeks of the war** *(Punka Archiv)*

This Bf 109G-14 was assigned to Lt Antal Szebeni of 101/4 FS in early 1945. On 18 February he shot down an La-5 west of Ipolyszalka while flying Bf 109G-14 W-0+60 (*Punka Archiv*)

Missions were halted due to bad weather on the 23rd, and no further flying took place in February. By month-end the Soviets had given up the Garam river bridgehead over which the Hungarians had fought so often.

At 1430 hrs on 1 March eight aircraft from 101/8 FS were scrambled to intercept a lone B-24 flying heading for Italy. Whilst in the process of taking off, the canopy of one of the Bf 109s came off, and another fighter hit it and flipped over. Within ten minutes the remaining six fighters had caught up with the bomber, 1/Lt Máthé's flight spotting it over Tótvázsony. Máthé's first burst set the bomber's right inner engine alight and knocked out the right radiator. Four of the crew bailed out over Lake Balaton, and the burning Liberator belly-landed 17 kms south-east of Sárvár, giving its victor his fifth kill. No further missions were then flown until 6 March due to another prolonged period of bad weather.

During this enforced lull in activity, 101/I and 101/III FGs were reorganised into one unit, 101/1 FS being joined by 101/7 FS, 101/2 FS being paired with 101/8 FS and 101/3 FS teaming up with 101/9 FS.

At around this time an order also came through from the Luftwaffe that the Royal Hungarian Air Force must display a serial number and individual markings on all of its aircraft. Furthermore, the theatre markings (yellow wing tips and fuselage band) had to be replaced with new theatre markings consisting of a yellow front engine cowling and rudder.

Despite continuing bad weather, the Germans embarked on Operation *Frühlingserwachsen* in Transdanubia. Troops had to contend with roads clogged with mud, and these boggy conditions also had a detrimental impact on 101 FW as well. Yet despite wet airfields, Soviet pilots were still active, the 17th Air Army flying 358 sorties on 6 March alone. The performances of the 3rd Guards Close-support Wing and the 3rd Guards Fighter Wing during this period were outstanding, and of the 358 sorties flown, 227 of them were directed against the 635th Panzer Army.

At the beginning of the new offensive the German-Hungarian forces had 850 aircraft in this sector, while the Soviets and Bulgarians had 965. The Soviet fighter airfields were between 40 and 50 kms behind the frontline, whilst the bombers were some 75 to 100 kms away.

On 8 March the combined 101/I and 101/III FGs were sent into action near Székesfehérvár, and the second flight of four aircraft sortied encountered eight Yak-9s over the city. The Hungarians were surprised by the new-found manoeuvrability of their opponents, but they nevertheless managed to prevail in their Bf 109G-10s, Ens Kálmán downing an aircraft south-east of Székesfehérvár. Lt Holéczy also set fire to an observation balloon discovered nearby.

At 1550 hrs Capt Pottyondy led four machines aloft to relieve the previous flight. Minutes after arriving over the frontline, the Hungarians ran into a number of Il-2s, escorted by Yak-9s, between Soponya and Kálóz. Engaging the *Stormoviks* whilst they were in the process of conducting a low-level attack on Axis troops, Pottyondy claimed his 13th, and last, victory when he despatched an Il-2. Soviet flak evened the score shortly afterwards, however, when it brought down Lt Victor Inkey's 'White 4'. He bailed out over enemy territory.

That same day General Dessloch, commander of *Luftflotte* 4, decorated several Hungarian fighter pilots, including 9-kill ace Sgt Lajos Buday, scorer of the 'Pumas" 100th victory the previous summer. He was awarded the Iron Cross, Second Class.

On 9 March literally hundreds of Soviet Il-2s sortied in an attempt to counter the Axis offensive, attacking German armoured units and troop concentrations. A handful of fighters from 101/I and 101/III FGs took off to oppose them as best they could, and four Bf 109s from the first flight to reach the battlefield clashed with between ten and twelve La-5s and La-7s over Gárdony at a height of 3500 m. During the engagement the Soviets lost a solitary La-7 to Lt Tóth, which took his tally to 22.

The second flight, consisting of eight aircraft led by 1/Lt Máthé, was in the process of taking off at 1015 hrs when 16 Bostons attacked the airfield at Várpalota. Among other targets that were bombed, a German first aid post suffered a direct hit, killing 140 soldiers. The Hungarian Bf 109s caught up with the last two Bostons south of Csór and swiftly shot them down – one fell to Lt Málik (taking his score to 9.5 kills) and the other to Ens Asztalos. La-5s then intervened, and during a fierce dogfight Málik's W-1+71 was shot down south-east of Öskü. To the relief of his colleagues, the ace later turned up at his base on foot.

Eight aircraft of 101/3 FS took off at 1310 hrs to intercept 25 Bostons, escorted by 16 Yak-9s, that were reportedly bombing targets between Igal and Tab from high altitude. Spotting the enemy formation above Berhida, the Hungarians commenced a steady climb in order to intercept the Soviet formation. By the time they had reached the northern end of Lake Balaton, they were at 3000 m, and the Bostons were beginning to turn south for Igal when the 'Pumas' attacked.

On his first pass Lt Pintér, flying 'Blue 1', downed a bomber, but he was then set upon by several Soviet fighters. Despite being hit in the left wing, Pintér kept his cool and used the manoeuvrability of his Bf 109G-10 to get in behind his quarry. With the 'bit between his teeth', the Hungarian chased the Yak almost all the way back to Kaposvár, although he was unable to bring it down. Meanwhile, Lt Dániel and Cpl/Maj Ferenc Szőcs had enjoyed more success when they destroyed a Yak-9 apiece.

Later that same afternoon yet another patrol of eight fighters tangled with more Yak-9s over Kálóz, although the odds were equal this time. Ens Szentgyörgyi duly boosted his tally to 24.5 kills when he destroyed a Yak fighter north-west of Sárbogárd.

Hungarian fighter pilots had sortied 56 times on 9 March, and as a result of their efforts German ground forces had gained some territory. However, this sortie rate could not be kept up and the Axis offensive ran out of steam. Confirmation of this came with the arrival of daily situation reports from troops in the frontline, and from the pilots themselves.

With things going badly on the ground, Hungarian fighter pilots also began to find their authority in the air being challenged too with the appearance of more and more La-7s. Although Axis pilots could not easily identify the new Lavochkin fighters by their shape (they looked very similar to the older La-5s), the self-confidence and aggressiveness of their pilots, who felt their machines were a match for the Bf 109G-10, marked them out in combat.

Up until then, the only fighter that could out-perform the Bf 109G-10 in the skies over Hungary at altitudes of between 6000 and 10,000 m had been the P-51B/D. Now, the La-7 matched the *Gustav's* speed at low to medium altitude and, worst of all, it could turn more quickly. On the other hand, the Messerschmitt's rate of climb was better, as was the performance of its Daimler-Benz engine at higher altitudes.

On 11 March a further 40 sorties were flown by the same groups that had seen combat the previous day. The first engagement of the day was fought between eight Hungarian fighters and six Il-2s over Seregélyes and Adony. The fighters were flying at 6000 m when they spotted the enemy 4000 m below them. Diving on their opponents at high speed, the 101 FW machines destroyed two Ilyushins on their first pass, Lt Dániel's victim exploding in mid-air and the second machine bursting into flames after it was hit by a salvo fired by Ens Huszár.

The next kills were claimed by a trio of pilots from a four-aircraft flight that took off at 1411 hrs, although only the La-5 downed by Ens Szentgyörgyi was actually confirmed as having been destroyed.

During the course of the eight missions conducted on the 11th, Cpl/Maj Buday scored his eighth and ninth victories when he downed an Il-2 and an La-5. At 1733 hrs the day's scoring was brought to an end by 1/Lt Máthé when he destroyed an La-5 north of Pusztaszabolcs.

As the advancing Red Army gained more and more ground, the non-operational flying elements of the Royal Hungarian Air Force (flying schools and training squadrons) left the country to continue their training – sometimes as part of other units – in Germany.

On 13 March 54 fighters participated in 14 missions south of Lake Velencei. Once again the weather was less than ideal, with a cloud base down to 100 m in places, forcing aircraft to fly very low. Soviet flak units took full advantage of this, downing 1/Lt Málnássy and Lts Nemere and Holéczy (in 'Yellow 17'). All three pilots belly-landed in friendly territory and returned to their units unharmed.

On a more positive note, other pilots managed four kills, Ens Fábián of 101/2 FS claiming an Il-2 south-west of Pázmánd, 1/Lt Máthé of the 101/7 FS downing a Yak-9 south of Baracska, 1/Lt Málnássy of 101/8 FS getting a second Yak-9 south of Gárdony and squadronmate Lt Szenteleky accounting for a *Stormovik* south-west of Lake Velencei.

Early the following morning a Luftwaffe reconnaissance flight spotted communist troop movements between Bicske and Zámoly, and the Hungarians were ordered into the air to counter them.

His chest adorned with medals, Lt József Málik also wears lapel badges featuring 101 FW's 'Puma' and JG 53's 'spade' emblems. Málik was killed during a strafing attack by USAAF Mustangs on Raffelding airfield on 16 April 1945, the 10.5-kill ace being caught in the open when the 40 P-51s struck
*(Petrick via Punka)*

Conducting the second mission of the day, a four-aircraft flight from 101/7 FS, led by Ens Kálmán, attacked 18 'B-26 Marauders', escorted by four Yak-9s, at 3000 m. During the ten-minute combat which ensued, Kálmán shot a bomber down at Alsódabas for his 11th, and last, victory – this aircraft was almost certainly a Boston, for the Soviet Air Force was never supplied with B-26s.

Kálmán's flight was relieved by a formation of eight aircraft, whose pilots had been briefed to patrol over Simontornya and Ozora. Having reached this area, they were confronted by chequer-tailed Mustangs of the Fifteenth Air Force's 325th FG, escorting formations of B-24s and B-17s on their way back from an attack on Florisdorf. A number of P-38s were also in the area as well. With the Lightnings sticking close to the bombers, the Mustang pilots went looking for prey, and up to eight American fighters got into a dogfight with the Hungarians. Lt Forró successfully engaged P-51D 44-63360 and saw rounds from his 30 mm cannon thudding into its cockpit and fuselage. The Mustang crashed south of Ozora.

15 March was relatively quiet, with only a lone B-17 being shot down during the afternoon by a flight of four aircraft from 101/5 FS, Ens Ottó Fekete being credited with bringing it down. That same day 101/2 FS's Ens Dezsö Szentgyörgyi was nominated for the Officer's Gold Medal for Valour. The citation with the award described how Szentgyörgyi had served on the Eastern Front between 15 July 1942 and 8 September 1943, flying 142 missions and scoring six kills. On 1 April 1944 he had been assigned to the Home Defence Fighter Group, with whom he had flown 58 missions and scored 19 more victories, including four B-24s.

On the 16th the 2nd and 3rd Ukrainian Fronts began their push towards Vienna, a formation of 78 fighters providing cover above the forward units of the 46th Army as it advanced on Pápa-Sopron. The 7th Guards Army, meanwhile, was pushing towards Pozsony (now Bratislava), along with the left flank of the 53rd Army, on the north side of the Danube. They were protected from the air by the 500 aircraft of the 5th Air Army. At Lake Balaton, to the south, 837 aircraft of the 17th Air Army were also active.

The offensive had begun with enormous artillery and aerial bombardments, the 244th Bomber Division's Bostons, with aircraft of the 9th (mixed) Flying Corps of the 17th Air Army, being sent into action at 1430 hrs. German-Hungarian resistance was weak due to all lines of communication having been cut between the various command headquarters.

The first quartet of Bf 109s scrambled in response to this new offensive turned back when the leader's fighter developed engine trouble. A second flight of four Messerschmitts hastily departed at 1424 hrs and headed for an area north of Székesfehérvár. Shortly after 1505 hrs the Hungarians attacked a formation of ten Il-2s south of the city, and during the fight Lt Dániel downed a *Stormovik* to boost his tally to 6.5 kills. The ace's victim exploded mid-air, while two other aircraft were also shot down.

A later patrol of four fighters, led by Lt Málik, took on 20 Bostons and two Yak-9s over Magyaralmás at a height of 6000 m. A ten-minute clash at high altitude brought Málik his final kill of the war (taking his tally to 10.5 victories) when he downed a Yak-9 over Bia. Four Messerschmitts from 101/3 and 101/7 FSs subsequently got involved in a fruitless engagement with four La-7s north-west of Székesfehérvár, the leader of the second pair, together with his wingman, returning to base after his engine was hit. Capt Békássy and Cpl/Maj Ernő Kiss remained aloft, however, and the latter pilot claimed his sixth, and last, kill when he destroyed a Yak-9 north of Bicske.

Tempering this success was the loss of nine-victory ace Sgt Lajos Buday, who was killed in combat with still more La-7s near Urhida. Two other fighters, Cpl/Maj Nagy's 'Red 2' and Cpl/Maj Faludi's 'Red 13', were also hit several times during the combat. A short while later, at 1640 hrs, Lt Galambos' 'White 7' flipped over and was written off while taking off for the next patrol. The final Bf 109 lost on this day was that assigned to Lt Forró, who was forced to belly-land when his engine caught fire in flight.

On a more positive note, 101/2 FS's Lt Lajos Tóth was given a field promotion to 1st lieutenant, the citation accompanying his promotion stating that he had served on the Eastern Front between 2 July 1943 and 20 March 1944, then in the Home Defence Fighter Group from 1 April 1944. He had scored 22 victories between 25 September 1943 and 9 March 1945, 18 of which were Soviet aircraft and four American.

The German retreat from Székesfehérvár began within hours of the Soviet offensive being launched on 16 March. Despite the weather being intermittently cloudy, nothing stopped Russian air activity, and both Hungarian groups were flying again on the 18th. Fighting without scoring any kills, 101 FW lost Cpl/Maj Rétfalvi in 'Yellow 13' to La-7s, the pilot making a belly-landing at Dombóvár, where he was taken prisoner. Two more Bf 109s were lost in emergency landings after being hit by flak, and a third returned to base with battle damage. The Soviets' own reports put Hungarian losses on the 17th and 18th at five.

On the 19th more missions were flown, although the communists avoided contact by slipping into the clouds before the Hungarians could engage them. Late in the morning 1/Lt Máthé finally shot down a Yak-9 east of Csór, the fighter falling away in flames. His eighth, and last, victory was confirmed by Leutnant Düttmann of II./JG 52.

At 1500 hrs a large-scale encounter finally took place. Four machines, led by Ens Szentgyörgyi, had taken off a short while earlier, bound for Berhida. One pilot had immediately returned when his landing gear refused to retract, and within minutes the remaining trio of aircraft were attacking two Il-2s over Nádasladány. Szentgyörgyi hit one of them north-west of the village and it exploded in mid-air. A second Il-2 was also downed by Ens Fábián (taking his tally to 16.5 kills), the *Stormovik* hitting the ground north of Nádasladány. More Il-2s then appeared on the scene, but the Hungarians could not bring any of them down.

At 1540 hrs 30 Bostons, escorted by ten La-5s and Yak-9s, entered the area. By then short of both fuel and ammunition, the 'Pumas' could make only one pass at them before heading back to base. Despite only briefly engaging the second formation, Szentgyörgyi reported a 'probable' La-5 kill, while Lt Károly Sipos thought he had got a Yak-9.

At about the same time eight machines from 101/7 FS engaged 12 Yak-9s over Osi – one of the Hungarian pilots soon departed the area when he found he could not jettison his drop-tank. The remaining seven scored three 'probable' kills, 1/Lt Máthé claiming a Yak and a Boston, while 1/Lt Vajda stated that he too had destroyed a Yak.

This Bf 109G-6/U2 of Cpl/Maj Károly Faludi suffered a collapsed undercarriage during a heavy landing at Veszprém in early March 1945. He was flying another aircraft – 'Red 13' – when it was hit several times during the 16 March combat with La-7s in which Sgt Lajos Buday was killed (*Zsák via Sinka*)

Just prior to midday on 20 March, eight members of 101/II FG were given the job of intercepting Il-2s spotted over Felsőgalla. Engaging the *Stormoviks* near Tatatóváros, the Hungarians attacked ten Il-2s that were being escorted by up to eight Yak-9s. Minutes later a further eight La-5s arrived on the scene, and the 101 FW pilots did well to escape unscathed.

That same day, at virtually the same time, eight more Bf 109s from 101/I and 101/II FGs intercepted 20 Bostons, escorted by a similar number of fighters, over Pátka-Sárkeresztúr. The engagement brought Ens Szentgyörgyi his 27th victory when his victim, flying an La-7, bailed out.

The 20th also saw 1/Lt Tóth score his 23rd victory above the airfield at Csór, although his opponent was not as lucky as Szentgyörgyi's – he went in with his Yak-9. Lt Forró also claimed a Yak-9 some six kilometres to the north-east, while 1/Lt Málnássy accounted for an Il-2 over Balatonkenese. There were no witnesses to the latter two victories so they were not confirmed, despite the Il-2 crashing in the centre of Balatonkenese! Also unconfirmed was Lt Michna's victory over a Yak-9, which he reported as having come down on the shore of Lake Tatai.

101/I FG closed the day's account with a victory by Lt Dániel after 16 Bostons and 20 Yak-3s were spotted over Várpalota. The ace increased his tally to 7.5 kills when he shot down the trailing Yak in the formation.

Aside from engaging enemy aircraft, 101/II FG's pilots had braved flak batteries to strafe vehicles advancing across farm land near Csákvár. The aircraft made a single low-level attack, knocking out eight trucks.

On 21 March Soviet troops commenced their push to capture Várpalota airfield. German and Hungarian troops were desperately defending it, trying to avoid being surrounded, and thus secure the withdrawal of forces from around Lake Velencei and Lake Balaton. Fierce combat took place overhead, with the first clash of the day seeing three Yak-9s that appeared overhead at 5500 m being swiftly despatched by eight Hungarian machines. Lt Dániel claimed his final victory when his target went down in flames, its pilot bailing out – as did the Russian flying the fighter claimed by Cpl/Maj Szőcs.

At 1153 hrs eight Bf 109s from 101/9 FS took off to engage Il-2s supporting the troops moving on Várpalota. However, they intercepted 17 Bostons and 25 fighters directly over the airfield at a height of 3000 m instead, Lt Szőts shooting down a Yak-3 in flames. Minutes later the

Soviet fighters got their revenge when Cpl/Maj Szilágyi, flying 'Yellow 9', went missing.

That afternoon 101/II FG was ordered to patrol between Mácsa, Nagyigmánd, Tata and Kocs, where Il-2s were known to be active. Soon after reaching the area, the Hungarians spotted 29 Yak-9s escorting 12 Il-2s. In this, the last mission to be flown by the wing from its traditional 'Puma Quarters' at Veszprém, Lt Nánási shot down a Yak-9 for his eighth kill. 101 FW suffered a grievous loss that evening when 11-kill ace 1/Lt Ferenc Málnássy died at the controls of an Fw 58 Weihe communications aircraft which was bounced by Lightnings and shot down.

On 23 March more missions were flown from Kenyeri, four fighters, led by 1/Lt Tóth, departing mid-morning. Encountering two Yak-3s, Ens Szentgyörgyi shot one down for his penultimate victory. Just prior to the departure of Tóth's flight, eight aircraft had sortied on a patrol bound for Siófok. With one of the fighters turning back straight after take-off, the rest headed for the southern shore of Lake Balaton, where they attacked 24 Bostons that were being escorted by just two Yak-9s. 101/5 FS scored several victories without any losses, Lt Nánási and Cpl/Maj Kérges each claiming a Yak-9, while Lts Báthy and Nyári and Ens Fekete all downed Bostons.

23 March had seen 101/III FG begin to operate independently once again, with four of its machines from 101/7 FS encountering several Mustangs at 5200 m south of Kisbér. The pilots could not engage the USAAF fighters, however, due to insufficient fuel.

The Soviet Air Force continued to increase its pressure on German forces, and on the 25th 101 FW was ordered to evacuate Kenyeri for Szombathely-Vát. A possible move further west to Grosspetersdorf, in Austria, was also considered, but the airfield there was already over-crowded with Luftwaffe aircraft. A group of 16 fighters, ready for combat, remained in Kenyeri, while the rest of the Bf 109s were evacuated. The pilots had to land in darkness at bomb-cratered Szombathely-Vát, resulting in no fewer than 26 machines being written off. Amazingly, there were no injuries.

After a brief lull to make good the carnage of 25 March, the number of missions increased again on 3 April. The airspace the Hungarians had been allocated to patrol was mainly over Vienna and Bratislava, and at first two aircraft would be sent up to check the enemy's positions. 101/I and 101/II FGs would then sortie a handful of fighters for low-level attack operations. The Bf 109s strafed infantry and cavalry columns, trucks and horse-drawn wagons on the roads between Vienna and the River Leitha, enduring the heavy defensive fire from the troops under attack. West of the river they enjoyed more success when they knocked out up to ten trucks and blew up an ammunition train.

101/III FG continued these attacks into the late afternoon of the 3rd, but eventually paid a heavy price. Lt József Gáspárfalvy of 101/3 FS belly-landed 'Blue 7' in enemy territory and Lt László Bajza from 101/1 FS went missing in W-2+16, as did Ens Sándor Berényi in 'Red 2'. The latter pilot rejoined his squadron the following day.

On 4 April 101/II FG was sent into action first when, at 0745 hrs, six of its pilots took off for a low-level strafing attack. Encountering heavy flak, and avoiding combat with eight La-5s, they succeeded in destroying

1/Lt Ferenc Málnássy of 102/2 FS claimed 11 confirmed victories between October 1944 and March 1945. All of his kills were scored against Soviet aircraft. Málnássy was killed on 21 March 1945 when the Fw 58 communications aircraft he was flying was bounced and shot down by a flight of P-38s
(Punka Archiv)

a number of horse-drawn wagons between Trauskirchen and Sollenau. Cpl/Maj Pál Fülüp was shot down by Soviet flak 15 kms south of Himberg, his Messerschmitt exploding when it hit the ground.

The next victim of these hazardous low-level operations was 9-kill ace Lt Kálmán Nánási, who was downed at 1640 hrs between Baden and Kattenbrunn – his aircraft hit a railway embankment and exploded. He had been one of 101/5 FS's most successful pilots, scoring all of his kills between December 1944 and March 1945. The final loss of the day was 1/Lt Füleki, who went missing south of Malacky.

Low-level attacks continued the following day, and an order came through during the afternoon for 101 FW to retreat to Raffelding. Over the previous few days four pilots had been killed in action, four listed missing in action and ten aircraft destroyed. Meanwhile, enemy troops were advancing along the roads toward Tulln. They met no German troops and saw no tanks.

The wing received new fighters to make up for its losses of early April, but because of fuel shortages each group was reduced to just 16 aircraft. Surplus pilots were sent to holding camps further away from the front.

Along with the arrival of new aircraft came new radio call signs and group identification letters. The new groups were 101/1 'Mátyás' (Matthew - Fighter Group Radio Code), with code letters 'White 1' to '16', 101/2 'Imre' (Emerich - Fighter Group Radio Code), with code letters 'Black 1' to '16', and 101/3 'János' (John - Fighter Group Radio Code), with code letters 'Yellow 1' to '16'.

On 8 April, after returning from a low-level attack, several fighters from 101/1 FG were ordered to take off again to intercept an RAF Mosquito. The reconnaissance aircraft put up a fight, turning on its pursuers and firing at them before escaping unscathed.

More missions followed the following day, when all three groups took off, one after the other, to perform more low-level attacks, or to tackle patrolling enemy fighters. Heavy flak followed their every move.

On the 13th 101/3 FG sortied first, and its eight fighters, led by 5-kill ace 1/Lt Kiss, came face-to-face with an identical number of Il-2s, escorted by ten La-5s and 16 Yak-9. The Soviet aircraft were attacking targets in Alsdorf, north-west of Vienna. Lt Nyári scored his second victory when he got in behind an La-5 at a height of 1200 m and his rounds found their mark. The Soviet fighter exploded and went down, its pilot unable to bail out. A few minutes later a Yak-9 was set on fire by Lt Pál Balogh, but its pilot was luckier than his colleague and he managed to abandon the machine. Cpl/Maj Kérges also shot down an La-5.

That afternoon eight more Hungarian Bf 109s (this time from 101/1 FG) took off and headed for Vienna. The flight ran into between 30 and 40 Yak-9s and La-7s north of the Austrian capital, and at 1735 hrs 1/Lt Tóth downed an La-7 in flames, killing the pilot. This success took the ace's tally to 24 victories.

Seven aircraft from 101/3 FG performed the final patrol of the day, attacking Bostons north-east of Vienna. Minutes later Ens Kálmán's 12th, and last, aerial kill of the war duly went down in flames south-east of Vienna, exploding on impact with the ground.

From 14 April the wing was forced to go into action in mixed formations because none of the groups now had enough fighters to operate as individual units. Just after noon eight machines, led by 1/Lt Tóth and 1/Lt Szénássy, took off into the haze. One aircraft soon returned because of landing gear trouble, while the rest were fighting it out with 12 Il-2s and six Yak-9s within half an hour. Both Tóth and Szénássy each claimed two Il-2s destroyed, although these successes came at a high price for four Bf 109s were lost and two pilots killed.

On the 16th a formation took off around noon for the Sankt-Pölten area, and the Hungarians were attacked by a mixed force of ten La-7s and Yak-9s east of Hofstedten. In a vicious encounter Ens Szentgyörgyi shot down a Yak-9, this proving to be his final kill of the war. That same day USAAF fighters attacked airfields in southern Germany.

The Hungarians were returning from their third mission of the day when Mustangs bounced them near the perimeter of their airfield. Another eight Messerschmitts were in the process of taking off, and these were pounced on by 16 fighters. Despite being hopelessly outnumbered, the Hungarians tried to fight it out, and a single P-51 was destroyed by Ens Béla Sőrő. His triumph was to be short-lived, however, for he was shot down seconds later by the wingman of the downed Mustang pilot. Four other 'Pumas' were also lost, as was 'White 16' (Wk-Nr 612775) parked on the ground. At least 20 other machines were damaged. Perhaps the greatest loss to the unit was that of 10.5-kill ace Lt József Málik, who was fatally wounded on the ground. According to USAAF records, the airfield had endured three low-level attacks by as many as 40 P-51s.

The 'Pumas'' final victory in World War 2 was scored by 1/Lt Kiss on 17 April, when he destroyed one of seven Yak-9s that his flight had encountered over Milowitz. This took his tally to six kills.

The following day most of the wing's surviving fighters were sent to Hörsching, and from there they flew more missions.

On the 23rd a handful of new Bf 109s were delivered, and these were distributed among the groups, but by now it was too late. These machines were destined never to see combat. Two days later Raffelding was subjected to yet another low-level attack by P-51s, which destroyed six more aircraft. Some of these were quickly replaced by aircraft ferried in by Hungarian pilots from Hörsching.

The 28th saw the last two new Bf 109s arrive at Raffelding, Wk-Nr 611022 going to 101/1 FG and Wk-Nr 163759 being allocated to 101/2 FG. On 1 May 1945 the final 101 FW communiqué revealed that the wing had just eight combat-ready fighters, although in reality 33 white-crossed Bf 109G-10s were dispersed around the airfield, and some of these were taken over by German pilots from other units.

Three days later the American vanguard reached Raffelding, and the 'Pumas' blew up their last unserviceable aircraft to prevent them falling into enemy hands.

This MG 131 13 mm machine gun was stripped out of a damaged Bf 109G and hastily mounted on the back of a truck to act as a mobile flak unit for the defence of Raffelding airfield in the last weeks of the war. Like most bases in southern Germany and Austria, this airfield was attacked on several occasions by marauding P-51s during the course of April and early May 1945 *(Punka Archiv)*

# APPENDICES

## Hungarian aces

### Ens Dezső Szentgyörgyi

*Awards*
Hungarian Knight's Cross
Hungarian Knight's Cross with War Ribbon and Swords
Bronze Medal of Valour
Small Silver Medal of Valour
Great Silver Medal of Valour (three times)
Officer's Gold Medal of Valour
Fire Cross, 1st Class
Small Silver Medal of Valour with War Ribbon and Swords
German Iron Cross, 1st Class
German Iron Cross, 2nd Class

| Kill type | Date | Location |
|---|---|---|
| Yak-1 | 26/6/43 | Gresnoje |
| Il-2 | 3/7/43 | Soviet Union |
| La-5 | 7/7/43 | Belgorod |
| La-5 | 3/8/43 | W of Belgorod |
| Il-2 | 3/8/43 | Belgorod |
| La-5 | 4/8/43 | S of Belgorod |
| Pe-2 | 4/8/43 | SW Of Belgorod |
| P-38 | 14/6/44 shared | Vérteskozma |
| P-51 | 27/6/44 | Márianostra |
| B-24 | 2/7/44 | Etyek |
| B-24 | 16/7/44 | Gálos |
| B-24 | 27/7/44 | Oroszlány |
| B-24 | 22/8/44 | Zalaerdőd |
| Yak-9 | 13/11/44 | Jászkisér |
| Il-2 | 16/11/44 | Albertfalu |
| Yak-9 | 8/12/44 | Érd-Martonvásár |
| Il-2 | 20/12/44 | Medgyespuszta |
| La-5 | 4/1/45 | SE of Bicske |
| La-5 | 8/1/45 | Szabadbattyán |
| La-5 | 18/1/45 | E of Aba |
| Il-2 | 18/1/45 | E of Polgárdi |
| Yak-9 | 28/1/45 | Kiskunlacháza |
| Yak-9 | 30/1/45 | N of Buda |
| Il-2 | 12/2/45 | NW of Budapest |
| Yak-9 | 9/3/45 | NW of Sárbogárd |
| La-5 | 11/3/45 | E of Sárbogárd |
| Il-2 | 19/3/45 | N of Nádasladány |
| La-5 | 19/3/45 | Balatonfőzfő |
| La-7 | 20/3/45 | NW of Sárkeresztúr |
| Yak-3 | 23/3/45 | NE of Tarján |
| Yak-9 | 16/4/45 | Guttenbrunn |

### 1/Lt György Debrődy

*Awards*
Hungarian Knight's Cross with War Ribbon and Swords
Hungarian Order of Officer's Cross with Swords
Hungarian Medal of Valour in Gold
Southland Medal for Merit
Transsylvanian Medal for Merit
German Iron Cross 1st Class
German Iron Cross 2nd Class

| Kill type | Date | Location |
|---|---|---|
| La-5 | 7/5/43 | Soviet Union |
| Il-2 | 7/7/43 | Soviet Union |
| Il-2 | 3/8/43 | Soviet Union |
| Yak-1 | 5/8/43 | Soviet Union |
| Il-2 | 6/8/43 | Soviet Union |
| Yak-1 | 8/8/43 | Soviet Union |
| Il-2 | 29/11/43 | Soviet Union |
| Yak-9 | 1/12/43 | Soviet Union |
| Il-2 | 14/12/43 | Shitomir |
| Il-2 | 1/1/44 | Vinniza |
| La-5 | 5/1/44 | Soviet Union |
| La-5 | 11/1/44 | Soviet Union |
| Il-2 | 11/1/44 | Soviet Union |
| Yak-1 | 25/1/44 | Soviet Union |
| La-5 | 27/1/44 | Soviet Union |
| La-5 | 1/2/44 | Soviet Union |
| Il-2 | 16/2/44 | Soviet Union |
| Il-2 | 16/2/44 | Soviet Union |
| P-38 | 14/6/44 | E of Dudar |
| P-38 | 16/6/44 | Kapoly |
| P-51 | 2/7/44 | Pilisvörösvár |
| B-17 | 7/7/44 shared | Megyercs |
| B-24 | 27/7/44 | Mór |
| B-24 | 5/11/44 not confirmed | unknown |
| La-5 | 16/11/44 | SE of Jászberény |
| Yak-9 | 16/11/44 | N of Nagykáta |

### Lt Lajos Tóth

*Awards*
Fire Cross 1st Class with Chaplet and Swords
Signum Laudis with War Ribbon and Swords (two times)
Hungarian Knight's Cross with War Ribbon and Swords
Hungarian Order of Officer's Cross with War Ribbon

and Swords
German Iron Cross 1st Class

| Kill type | Date | Location |
|---|---|---|
| La-5 | 5/9/43 | Senkow |
| Yak-1 | 15/9/43 | Kiew |
| Yak-1 | 25/9/43 | Over the Dnieper |
| Il-2 | 28/9/43 | Pereieslaw |
| Il-2 | 28/9/43 | Pereieslaw |
| Il-2 | 5/11/43 | Tsuguiew-Voltsansk |
| Il-2 | 6/11/43 | Shitomir |
| Il-2 | 29/11/43 | Shitomir |
| La-5 | 15/1/44 | Sosovo-Vasnievka |
| P-39 | 27/2/44 | Kirowograd |
| P-51 | 16/6/44 | W of Felsőireg |
| B-17 | 27/6/44 | Szentendre |
| P-38 | 7/7/44 | Tét |
| B-24 | 5/11/44 | N of Iharos |
| Yak-9 | 13/11/44 | Tápiószele |
| Il-2 | 16/11/44 | Apatin |
| Yak-9 | 5/12/44 | N of Örkény |
| Yak-9 | 9/12/44 | Györköny |
| La-5 | 4/1/45 | SE of Bicske |
| Yak-9 | 23/1/45 | Lovasberény |
| La-5 | 23/1/45 | Ercsi |
| La-7 | 9/3/45 | SE of Gárdony |
| Yak-9 | 20/3/45 | N of Csór |
| La-7 | 13/4/45 | N of Wien |
| Il-2 | 14/4/45 | NE of Wien |
| Il-2 | 14/4/45 | Hauslenten |

### Lt László Molnár (posthumous 1/Lt)

**Awards**
Hungarian Knight's Cross with War Ribbon and Swords
Hungarian Silver Medal for Merit with War Ribbon
and Swords
Fire Cross 1st Class with Chaplet and Swords
Hungarian Silver Medal for Merit with Crown and War
Ribbon and Swords
Hungarian Medal of Valour in Gold
German Iron Cross 1st Class
German Iron Cross 2nd Class

| Kill type | Date | Location |
|---|---|---|
| ? | 3/8/43 | Soviet Union |
| ? | 16/8/43 | Soviet Union |
| Yak-1 | 8/9/43 | Soviet Union |
| Il-2 | 7/10/43 | Soviet Union |
| La-5 | 7/10/43 | Soviet Union |
| ? | 7/10/43 | Soviet Union |
| ? | to 29/10/43 four more victories (USSR) | |
| Il-2 | 8/1/44 | Sugatsova |
| Il-2 | 8/1/44 | Sugatsova |

| Il-2 | 8/1/44 | Sugatsova |
|---|---|---|
| La-5 | 8/1/44 | Sugatsova |
| ? | End of 1/44 | Soviet Union |
| ? | End of 1/44 | Soviet Union |
| ? | Beginning of 2/44 | Soviet Union |
| P-38 | 14/6/44 | N of Pusztavám |
| B-24 | 7/7/44 | Kolozsnéma |
| B-24 | 7/7/44 | Megyercs |
| B-24 | 26/7/44 | German territory |
| B-24 | 27/7/44 | Csákvár |
| B-24 | 30/7/44 shared | Nádasladány |

### Lt Miklós Kenyeres
(only partly known, total 18 victories)

**Awards**
Hungarian Order of Knight's Cross with War Ribbon
and Swords
Small Silver Medal of Valour
Hungarian Gold Medal for Courage
Fire Cross 1st Class
German Iron Cross 1st Class
German Iron Cross 2nd Class

| Kill type | Date | Location |
|---|---|---|
| Il-2 | 5/7/43 | Soviet Union |
| La-5 | 7/10/43 | Soviet Union |
| La-5 | 7/10/43 | Soviet Union |
| Yak-9 | 1/2/44 | Soviet Union |

### Ens István Fábián

**Awards**
Southland Medal for Merit
Transsylvanian Medal for Merit
Small Silver Medal of Valour (two times)
Great Silver Medal of Valour
Bronze Medal of Valour
Fire Cross 1st Class
German Iron Cross 1st Class
German Iron Cross 2nd Class

| Kill type | Date | Location |
|---|---|---|
| ? | 16/6/43 | Soviet Union |
| Yak-1 | 26/6/43 | Gresnoje |
| Il-2 | 3/7/43 | N of Belgorod |
| ? | 7/7/43 | Soviet Union |
| Il-2 | 7/7/43 probable | Soviet Union |
| ? | 3/8/43 probable | Soviet Union |
| ? | 4/8/43 probable | Soviet Union |
| ? | 6/8/43 probable | Soviet Union |
| ? | 9/8/43 probable | Soviet Union |
| Il-2 | 28/9/43 | Pereszlav |

| | | |
|---|---|---|
| La-5 | 28/9/43 | Pereszlav |
| ? | 28/10/43 probable | Soviet Union |
| P-38 | 14/6/44 shared | N of Pusztavám |
| B-24 | 30/6/44 | Veszprémpinkóc |
| Yak-9 | 13/11/44 | S of Tápiószele |
| La-5 | 20/12/44 | near Érd |
| Pe-2 | 16/1/45 | N of Pincehely |
| Yak-9 | 16/1/45 | Sárszentmihály |
| La-5 | 16/1/45 | Sárszentmihály |
| La-5 | 19/2/45 | Tardos |
| La-5 | 19/2/45 | Tardos |
| Il-2 | 13/3/45 | SW of Pázmánd |
| Il-2 | 19/3/45 | N of Nádasladány |

## Capt László Pottyondy

### Awards
Hungarian Bronze Medal for Merit with Crown
Hungarian Silver Medal for Merit with Crown
Hungarian Order of Knight's Cross
Hungarian Order of Officer's Cross with War Ribbon
and Swords
Southland Medal for Merit
Transsylvanian Medal for Merit
Northland Medal for Merit
German Iron Cross 1st Class
German Iron Cross 2nd Class
Frontflugspange in Gold

| Kill type | Date | Location |
|---|---|---|
| I-16 | 12/7/41 | Dunajewci |
| Il-2 | 15/9/44 | Mezőlaborc |
| La-5 | 9/10/44 | Tuchla |
| Boston | 30/10/44 | Kiskörös |
| Yak-9 | 30/10/44 | Törökszentmiklós |
| La-5 | 1/11/44 | Szolnok |
| Boston | 17/11/44 | Ócsa |
| Il-2 | 22/12/44 | Csány |
| Yak-9 | 3/1/45 | Csapdi |
| Boston | 14/1/45 | Pilisvörösvár |
| La-5 | 22/1/45 | Ercsi |
| Yak-9 | 20/2/45 | Szendehely |
| Il-2 | 8/3/45 | Kálóz |

## 1/Lt István Kálmán

### Awards
Hungarian Bronze Medal for Merit with Crown
Hungarian Silver Medal for Merit with Crown
German Iron Cross 1st Class
German Iron Cross 2nd Class
Frontflugspange in Silver

| Kill type | Date | Location |
|---|---|---|
| Il-2 | 14/9/44 | Sanok |
| Obs balloon | 14/9/44 | over the Carpatian |
| La-5 | 30/10/44 | Rákóczyfalva |
| Boston | 1/11/44 | Cegléd |
| Yak-9 | 5/12/44 | Hatvan |
| Il-2 | 14/12/44 | Balatonakarattya |
| Il-2 | 14/12/44 | Balatonakarattya |
| Il-2 | 22/1/45 | Bugyi |
| Il-2 | 22/1/45 | Bugyi |
| U-2 | 22/1/45 | Bugyi |
| Yak-9 | 8/3/45 | Dömsöd |
| Boston | 14/3/45 | Alsódabas |

## Lt József Málik

### Awards
Hungarian Order of Officer's Cross with War Ribbon
and Swords
Fire Cross 1st Class with Chaplet and Swords
Honourable Recognition on War Ribbon and Swords
German Iron Cross 1st Class
German Iron Cross 2nd Class

| Kill type | Date | Location |
|---|---|---|
| P-38 | 14/6/44 shared | N of Pusztavám |
| B-24 | 27/6/44 | S of Lake Balaton |
| B-17 | 27/6/44 | Island of Szentendre |
| P-51 | 7/8/44 | Ikervár |
| P-51 | 12/10/44 | Nádasladány |
| B-24 | 5/11/44 | SE of Nagykanizsa |
| Yak-9 | 3/1/45 | N of Gödöllő |
| La-5 | 23/1/45 | W of Üllő |
| Pe-2 | 2/2/45 | S of Ráckeresztúr |
| Boston | 9/3/45 | SE of Várpalota |
| Yak-9 | 16/3/45 | Bia |

## 1/Lt Ferenc Málnássy

### Awards
Hungarian Bronze Medal for Merit with Crown
Hungarian Silver Medal for Merit with Crown
German Iron Cross 1st Class
German Iron Cross 2nd Class

| Kill type | Date | Location |
|---|---|---|
| La-5 | 9/10/44 | Tuchla |
| Boston | 1/11/44 | Újkécske |
| Il-2 | 13/11/44 | Jászapáti |
| Il-2 | 5/12/44 | Hatvan |
| La-5 | 5/12/44 | Hatvan |
| Il-2 | 14/12/44 | Hatvan |
| Il-2 | 14/12/44 | Hatvan |

| | | |
|---|---|---|
| Boston | 14/1/45 | Csepel |
| La-5 | 14/1/45 | Baracska |
| La-5 | 14/1/45 | Baracska |
| La-5 | 13/3/45 | Seregélyes |
| Il-2 | 20/3/45 not confirmed | Balatonkonese |

## 1/Lt László Dániel

### Awards
Honourable Recognition on War Ribbon and Swords
Small Silver Medal of Valour with War Ribbon and Swords
Fire Cross 1st Class
German Iron Cross 2nd Class

| Kill type | Date | Location |
|---|---|---|
| P-38 | 14/6/44 shared | SE of Pusztavám |
| P-38 | 27/6/44 not confirmed | N of Budapest |
| P-38 | 2/7/44 | Enying |
| B-24 | 30/7/44 shared | Nádasladány |
| B-24 | 30/7/44 shared | Nádasladány |
| La-5 | 8/1/45 | Székesfehérvár |
| Yak-9 | 9/3/45 | Igal-Tab |
| Il-2 | 11/3/45 | Sárosd |
| Il-2 | 16/3/45 | S of Pátka |
| Yak-3 | 20/3/45 | Bakonycsernye |
| Yak-9 | 21/3/45 | Várpalota |

## 1/Lt László Máthé

### Awards
Southland Medal for Merit
Transsylvanian Medal for Merit
Northland Medal for Merit
Hungarian Bronze Medal for Merit with Crown and War
Ribbon and Swords
Hungarian Silver Medal for Merit with Crown and War
Ribbon and Swords
Fire Cross 1st Class
Hungarian Order of Knight's Cross with War Ribbon
and Swords
German Iron Cross 1st Class
German Iron Cross 2nd Class
Frontflugspange in Gold

| Kill type | Date | Location |
|---|---|---|
| Il-2 | 14/9/44 | SE of Sanok |
| La-5 | 10/12/44 | W of Mezőtur |
| Yak-9 | 21/12/44 | SW of Székesfehérvár |
| Yak-9 | 22/12/44 | N of Bugyi |
| B-24 | 1/3/45 | SE of Székesfehérvár |
| La-5 | 11/3/45 | NE of Pusztaszabolcs |
| Yak-9 | 13/3/45 | SE of Baracska |
| Yak-9 | 19/3/45 | E of Csór |

| | | |
|---|---|---|
| Yak-3 | 19/3/45 probable | S of Várpalota |
| Boston | 19/3/45 probable | Siófok |

## Lt Kálmán Nánási

### Awards
Hungarian Bronze Medal for Merit with Crown and War
Ribbon and Swords
Hungarian Silver Medal for Merit with Crown and War
Ribbon and Swords
Fire Cross 1st Class
Honourable Recognition
German Iron Cross 2nd Class

| Kill type | Date | Location |
|---|---|---|
| La-5 | 24/12/44 | Esztergom |
| Il-2 | 2/1/45 | Esztergom |
| Il-2 | 2/1/45 | Esztergom |
| Yak-9 | 3/1/45 | Bicske |
| Il-2 | 22/1/45 | SW of Szigetszentmiklós |
| Il-2 | 22/1/45 | Székesfehérvár |
| La-5 | 4/2/45 | NW of Ladánybene |
| Yak-9 | 21/3/45 | Tata |
| Yak-9 | 23/3/45 | S of Siófok |

## Sgt Lajos Buday

### Awards
Small Silver Medal of Valour
Great Silver Medal of Valour
German Iron Cross 1st Class
German Iron Cross 2nd Class

| Kill type | Date | Location |
|---|---|---|
| B-24 | 26/6/44 | Balozsameggyes |
| B-24 | 22/8/44 | Tapolca |
| B-24 | 5/11/44 | Pusztamagyaród |
| Boston | 17/11/44 | N of Solt |
| La-5 | 3/1/45 | Pázmánd |
| Yak-9 | 16/1/45 | Seregélyes |
| Yak-9 | 19/1/45 | NW of Tolna |
| Il-2 | 11/3/45 | Sárkeresztúr |
| La-5 | 11/3/45 | W of Adony |

## Lt Col Aladár Heppes

### Awards
Hungarian Order of Officer's Cross with War Ribbon
and Swords
Small Silver Medal of Valour
Great Silver Medal of Valour
Fire Cross 1st Class

Southland Medal for Merit
Transsylvanian Medal for Merit
Northland Medal for Merit
German Iron Cross 1st Class
German Iron Cross 2nd Class

| Kill type | Date | Location |
|---|---|---|
| Yak-1 | 30/5/43 | Kupiansk |
| Yak-1 | 30/5/43 | Kupiansk |
| Il-2 | 6/7/43 | Woltsansk |
| Yak-1 | 3/8/43 | Belgorod |
| B-24 | 26/6/44 | Nagyacsád |
| B-24 | 26/6/44 | Mosonszolnok |
| B-17 | 2/7/44 | Pusztaszabolcs |
| B-24 | 7/7/44 | Hajmáskér |

### Capt György Újszászy

**Awards**

Honourable Recognition on War Ribbon and Swords
Hungarian Bronze Medal for Merit
Hungarian Silver Medal for Merit
Fire Cross 1st Class
German Iron Cross 1st Class
German Iron Cross 2nd Class

| Kill type | Date | Location |
|---|---|---|
| I-17 | 27/8/41 | Uljanovka |
| I-17 | 27/8/41 | Uljanovka |
| Il-2 | 27/4/43 | Soviet Union |
| Il-2 | 28/4/43 | Soviet Union |
| La-5 | 7/7/43 probable | Soviet Union |
| Il-2 | 13/7/43 | Soviet Union |
| Il-2 | 13/7/43 | Soviet Union |
| Pe-2 | 1/8/43 | N of Belgorod |
| B-24 | 3/4/44 shared | Budapest |

### Lt György Michna

**Awards**

Hungarian Bronze Medal for Merit with Crown and War Ribbon and Swords
Hungarian Silver Medal for Merit with Crown and War Ribbon and Swords
Fire Cross 1st Class with Wounding Ribbon
German Iron Cross 1st Class
German Iron Cross 2nd Class

| Kill type | Date | Location |
|---|---|---|
| B-24 | 5/11/44 | SW of Balaton |
| Yak-9 | 8/12/44 | E of Kápolnásnyék |
| La-5 | 8/12/44 | N of Velence |
| Yak-9 | 19/1/45 | NW of Tolna |

| Yak-9 | 12/2/45 | S of Nagykáta |
|---|---|---|
| Yak-9 | 12/2/45 | N of Dunaharaszti |
| Yak-9 | 20/3/45 not confirmed | Sea of Tata |

### Lt Imre Pánczél

**Awards**

Knight's Cross of the Hungarian Order with War Ribbon and Swords
Southland Medal for Merit
Transsylvanian Medal for Merit
Northland Medal for Merit
Small Silver Medal for Merit of Valour
Fire Cross 1st Class

| Kill type | Date | Location |
|---|---|---|
| Il-2 | 29/10/42 | Podgornoje |
| Il-2 | 30/10/42 | Kamenka |
| Il-2 | 31/10/42 | Soviet Union |
| Il-2 | 16/12/42 | Soviet Union |
| Il-2 | 16/12/42 | Soviet Union |
| Il-2 | 16/12/42 | Soviet Union |
| Il-2 | 16/12/42 | Soviet Union |

### 1/Lt József Bejczy

**Awards**

Southland Medal for Merit
Northland Medal for Merit
Hungarian Order of Knight's Cross with War Ribbon and Swords
Fire Cross 1st Class
Honourable Recognition
German Iron Cross 2nd Class

| Kill type | Date | Location |
|---|---|---|
| Yak-1 | 6/7/43 | Woltsansk |
| Boston | 9/7/43 | Kursk |
| Il-2 | 19/7/43 | Kursk |
| Pe-2 | 1/8/43 | N of Belgorod |
| P-38 | 16/6/44 | SW of Értény |
| B-24 | 16/7/44 | Kenyeri |

### 1/Lt Pál Irányi

**Awards**

Hungarian Order of Knight's Cross with War Ribbon and Swords
Fire Cross 1st Class with two Wounding Ribbons
Southland Medal for Merit
Transsylvanian Medal for Merit
Northland Medal for Merit

Honourable Recognition on War Ribbon and Swords
German Iron Cross of the 1st Class

| Kill type | Date | Location |
|---|---|---|
| LaGG-3 | 10/8/42 | Davidovka |
| Il-2 | 2/9/42 | Area of Korotojak |
| B-17 | 3/4/44 | N of Ferihegy |
| B-24 | 13/4/44 | N of Ferihegy |
| P-38 | 26/6/44 | N of Tés |
| B-24 | 2/7/44 | Felsöörs |
| B-24 | 2/7/44 shared | Petten-puszta |

## Sgt Ernő Kiss

### Awards
Small Silver Medal of Valour
Great Silver Medal of Valour
Hungarian Bronze Medal for Merit of Valour
Fire Cross 1st Class
German Iron Cross 2nd Class

| Kill type | Date | Location |
|---|---|---|
| Il-2 | 8/1/43 | Sugatsova |
| Il-2 | 8/1/43 | Sugatsova |
| La-5 | 8/1/44 | E of Sugovachowka |
| Il-2 | 8/1/44 | E of Sugovachowka |
| La-5 | 15/8/44 | E of Opatov |
| Yak-9 | 17/4/45 | N of Bicske |

## Sgt Pál Kovács

### Awards
Small Silver Medal of Valour
Great Silver Medal of Valour
Hungarian Bronze Medal of Valour
Fire Cross 1st Class

| Kill type | Date | Location |
|---|---|---|
| Il-2 | 5/7/43 | unknown |
| Il-2 | 5/7/43 | unknown |
| ? | 10/43 | unknown |
| ? | 10/43 | unknown |
| P-38 | 16/6/44 | Balatonkereki |
| B-24 | 30/7/44 shared | Nádasladány |

## Lt Kálmán Szeverényi

### Awards
Hungarian Order of Knight's Cross with War Ribbon
and Swords
Hungarian Bronze Medal for Merit
Hungarian Silver Medal for Merit

Signum Laudis
Fire Cross 1st Class
German Iron Cross 2nd Class

| Kill type | Date | Location |
|---|---|---|
| La-5 | 7/10/43 | Dnieper |
| Boston | 28/10/44 | Büdszentmihály |
| Il-2 | 11/11/44 | Kecskemét |
| Il-2 | 13/11/44 | Jászberény |
| B-17 | 13/2/45 | W of Bazsi |

## Cpl/Maj Mátyás Lőrincz

### Awards
Small Silver Medal of Valour
Great Silver Medal of Valour
Fire Cross 1st Class

| Kill type | Date | Location |
|---|---|---|
| P-38 | 16/6/44 | Balatonszántód |
| P-38 | 16/6/44 | Balatonszántód |
| P-38 | 16/6/44 (unofficial) | Balatonendréd |
| B-24 | 7/7/44 | Györgyszentmárton |
| P-51 | 12/10/44 | Aszófő |

## Lt Ervin Flóznik

### Awards
Hungarian Bronze Medal for Merit with Crown and War
Ribbon and Swords
Hungarian Silver Medal for Merit with Crown and War
Ribbon and Swords
Fire Cross 1st Class

| Kill type | Date | Location |
|---|---|---|
| ? | 1944 | unknown |
| ? | 1944 | unknown |
| ? | 1944 | unknown |
| Il-2 | 17/11/44 | Gyöngyös |
| Il-2 | 17/11/44 | Gyöngyös |

## Ens Sándor Hautzinger

### Awards
Not known

| Kill type | Date | Location |
|---|---|---|
| ? | 20/7/43 | Soviet Union |
| ? | 4/8/43 | Soviet Union |
| Yak-1 | 8/8/43 | Soviet Union |
| Il-2 | 10/8/43 | Kharkov |
| Il-2 | 5/9/43 | Soviet Union |

## Lt Mihály Karátsonyi

### Awards
Hungarian Bronze Medal for Merit
Fire Cross 1st Class
Honourable Recognition on War Ribbon with Swords
German Iron Cross 1st Class
German Iron Cross 2nd Class

| Kill type | Date | Location |
| --- | --- | --- |
| P-38 | 16/6/44 | Lake Balaton |
| P-38 | 14/7/44 | W of Budapest |
| P-38 | 14/7/44 | W of Budapest |
| B-24 | 27/7/44 | Szabadbattyán |
| P-51 | 7/8/44 | NW of Lake Balaton |

## Sgt Lajos Krascsenics

### Awards
Hungarian Bronze Medal for Merit
Great Silver Medal of Valour
German Iron Cross 2nd Class

| Kill type | Date | Location |
| --- | --- | --- |
| B-24 | 1/11/44 not confirmed | unknown |
| Yak-9 | 13/11/44 | Tápiószele |
| La-5 | 21/12/44 | Székesfehérvár |
| La-5 | 16/1/45 | W of Sárosd |
| Il-2 | 18/1/45 | E of Polgárdi |

## Cpl/Maj János Mátyás

### Awards
Hungarian Bronze Medal for Merit with War Ribbon
and Swords
Southland Medal for Merit
Transsylvanian Medal for Merit
Great Silver Medal of Valour
Small Silver Medal of Valour (two times)
Fire Cross 1st Class
German Iron Cross 2nd Class

| Kill type | Date | Location |
| --- | --- | --- |
| ? | 1943 | unknown |
| ? | 1943 | unknown |
| ? | 1943 | unknown |
| Il-2 | 3/8/1943 | unknown |
| P-38 | 16/6/1944 shared | NW of Értény |

## 1/Lt Tibor Papp

### Awards
Northland Medal for Merit
Transsylvanian Medal for Merit
Honourable Recognition on War Ribbon with Swords
Fire Cross 1st Class with War Ribbon amd Swords
Hungarian Bronze Medal for Merit with Crown with War
Ribbon and Swords
German Iron Cross 2nd Class

| Kill type | Date | Location |
| --- | --- | --- |
| La-5 | 7/7/43 | Belgorod-Woltsansk |
| Il-2 | 3/8/43 | W of Belgorod |
| La-5 | 5/8/43 | Belgorod |
| B-24 | 3/4/44 | Kulcs |
| B-24 | 22/8/44 probable | N of Balaton |

## 1

**Re.2000 *Heja* V.4+27 of Lt Imre Páncél, 1/1 'Dongó' (Wasp) FS, Staryj Oskol, Soviet Union, October 1942**
Páncél was the Royal Hungarian Air Force's premier ace, and his first three kills came in October 1942 while flying the obsolescent Re.2000. He was killed by Soviet flak on 11 January 1943 whilst flying a fighter-bomber mission in a Bf 109F-4/B.

## 2

**Bf 109F-4/B V-+07 of Sgt Dezső Szentgyörgyi, 1/1 FS, Rossosh, Soviet Union, early 1943**
Szentgyörgyi's first victory came in an Re.2000 *Heja*, when he saw a German He 111 mistakenly bombing Hungarian positions and thought it was an enemy raider. The Hungarians began to receive second-hand Bf 109Fs in late 1943, these being passed on to them from German repair depots. The first digit in the code system used by the Hungarians was initially left off of early Bf 109Fs, as this had been reserved for the He 112, which was due to enter service with the air force in 1943. The Heinkel fighters never materialised, however, and three-digit codes were applied to Bf 109s from the spring of 1943 onwards. The new style of national marking seen both on this machine and the Re.2000 in profile 1 was introduced in 1942 because the old pre-war red-white-green chevron insignia was not deemed to be visible enough in the heat of combat. This particular machine has had its original camouflage scheme temporarily overpainted in-the-field with winter white.

## 3

**Bf 109F-4/B 'Yellow 7' of Sgt Dezső Szentgyörgyi, 1/1 FS, Poltava, Soviet Union, late February 1943**
Generally, Hungarian aircraft assigned to German fighter units sported code numbers to make their identification easier. Due to 1/1 FS's aircraft strength rarely reaching operational requirements, each Bf 109 was routinely flown by more than one pilot. As weather conditions improved in 1943, so the winter camouflage became redundant and regulation markings were reapplied. The Hungarians were flying fighter-bomber missions at this time.

## 4

**Bf 109F-4/B V-+03 of 1/Lt György Debrődy, 5/1 FS, Uman, Soviet Union, Spring 1943**
The national markings and codes applied to the Bf 109s handed over to the Hungarians by the Germans were painted on in-the-field, hence their size, shape and positioning often varied. Many future aces who gained experience in low-level flying during fighter-bomber sorties in 1942–43 found later models of the Bf 109 less troublesome to fly than those pilots who had flown the F-model exclusively on fighter missions. György Debrődy claimed 18 victories whilst serving on the Eastern Front in 1943–44.

## 5

**Bf 109G-2 'Black H' of Lt Kálmán Szeverényi, 5/2 FS, Soviet Union, Spring 1943**
Szeverényi's early-build *Gustav* features only a partially marked tail and toned-down white crosses. Claiming an La-5 destroyed whilst still flying the Re.2000 on 10 October 1943, Szeverényi failed to add to his tally until late October 1944, by which time he was fighting the Soviet Air Force from Hungarian soil.

## 6

**Bf 109F-4/B V-0+39 of Maj Aladár Heppes, Group Commander of 5/I FG, Kharkov, Soviet Union, May 1943**
Heppes scored his first victories (two Yak-1s) in this machine on 30 May 1943 near Kupiansk. One of the first Bf 109s to feature the 'Pumas'' distinctive emblem on its cowling, this aircraft bears standard summer markings for the period. Heppes claimed four kills in the USSR in 1943, and later 'made ace' with the destruction of three B-24s and a single B-17 during the defence of Hungary in June–July 1944.

## 7

**Bf 109F-4/B V.0+41 of Sgt Pál Kovács, 5/2 FS, Varvasovka, Soviet Union, Summer 1943**
Kovács' Messerschmitt has yet to have its Hungarian tail stripes applied, the white fuselage and wing crosses usually being painted on in advance of the fin/rudder decoration. The fighter's spinner has been marked half-black and half-white, thus conforming to the non-standard schemes that adorned the spinners of most Hungarian Bf 109s throughout the war. Kovacs claimed four kills on the Eastern Front in 1943–44.

## 8

**Bf 109G-6 V-3+84 of Lt László Molnár, 5/2 FS, Varvasovka, Soviet Union, August 1943**
Molnár achieved 17 kills on the Eastern Front, opening his account with two unrecorded types in August 1943 whilst almost certainly flying this machine. By the end of October he had claimed ten victories, including a trio of kills on the 7th of that month. The leading Hungarian ace at that time, he was awarded the Iron Cross Second Class by the Germans in the autumn of 1943. Note how this particular machine has had its abbreviated Hungarian tail marking applied directly over a stencilled swastika.

## 9

**Bf 109F-4 'Red 2' of Sgt/Maj Dezső Szentgyörgyi, 1/1 FS, Kursk-East, Soviet Union, late 1943**
Due to the number of missions being flown by the 'Pumas' in mid to late 1943, there was often no time to repaint the German markings with Hungarian ones when replacement aircraft were issued to the unit. In many cases only the partially applied red-white-green national colours on the tail surfaces distinguished partly overpainted Hungarian fighters from German ones. Individual fighters would often change hands several times over after being repaired at servicing depots, Bf 109s re-deploying either to German, Hungarian or Rumanian units, depending on who required aircraft most urgently. Hungarian fighters did not sport any squadron emblems during this period. Sgt/Maj Szentgyörgi had claimed seven kills by the time he was issued with this machine.

## 10

**Bf 109G-6 'Black 66' of Lt László Molnár, 5/2 FS, Kalinovka, Soviet Union, early 1944**

Molnár scored his 17th, and last, victory on the Eastern Front in this winter-camouflaged aircraft in February 1944 – his operational records do not reveal the type of aircraft destroyed, or when it was shot down. One month earlier, on 8 January, he had claimed three Il-2s and an La-5 destroyed in a single mission, this feat never being repeated by a Hungarian pilot. His exploits earned him the Iron Cross First Class from the Germans, and made him the ranking Hungarian ace at the time. The severity of the winter weather in the USSR made it all but impossible for long-suffering Hungarian groundcrews to repaint Bf 109s handed over by the Germans during this period. Although this particular fighter had been assigned the code V3+66, there had been no time, or a spell of appropriate weather, in which to paint it on. Note the name *Erzsike* (Betty) painted immediately behind the canopy.

## 11

**Bf 109G-6 V3+73 of Lt Lajos Tóth, 5/2 FS, Uman, Soviet Union, February 1944**

Tóth flew 95 combat missions and achieved ten victories on the Eastern Front, the last of his successes in this theatre being a highly prized P-39 downed on 27 February 1944. This aircraft has again been only partially repainted.

## 12

**Bf 109G-6 V.8+22 of 1/Lt Pál Irányi, First Officer of 101/I 'Puma' FG, Veszprém, Hungary, May 1944**

One of the longest serving of all Hungarian fighter pilots, Pál Irányi's first combat missions were flown on the Eastern Front in 1941 in CR.42s and Re.2000s. Amongst the first pilots to be retrained on the Bf 109, he went on to complete 48 combat missions during two tours on the Eastern Front, claiming two victories (in the Re.2000) in the process. Returning to Hungary, Irányi scored four more kills with the 'Pumas' between April and July 1944. Indeed, he led the whole 'Puma' fighter group into action against American bomber formations on several occasions. This particular *Gustav* was one of 600-plus built under licence in Hungary.

## 13

**Bf 109G-6 (Gy.sz. 95 226) V.8+10 of Maj Aladár Heppes, Group Commander of 101/I FG, Veszprém, Hungary, May 1944**

The newly reformed 'Puma' fighter group, consisting of three squadrons, was the only unit available to defend Hungary from the USAAF onslaught in the spring of 1944. Dubbed the 'Old Puma' by his colleagues, 40-year-old Aladár Heppes achieved ace status during aerial clashes with American heavy bombers in June and July 1944.

## 14

**Bf 109G-6 (Gy.sz. 95 244) V.8+16 of 1/Lt József Bejczy, 101/3 'Puma' FS, Veszprém, Hungary, Summer 1944**

Another veteran of the Eastern Front in 1942–43, József Bejczy flew more than 100 combat missions during World War 2. He claimed four kills in the USSR and then 'made ace' by destroying a P-38 and a B-24 in mid 1944 while flying with the 'Pumas'. Eventually promoted to squadron commander, Bejczy was listed as missing in action on 4 November 1944 when he was downed by the defensive fire put up by a number of Red Army tanks that he was strafing near Szolnok, in Hungary.

## 15

**Bf 109G-6 V.8+48 of Lt László Molnár, 101/3 'Puma' FS, Veszprém, Hungary, July 1944**

Lászlo Molnar saw much action in this machine in July 1944, downing three B-24s with it. The fighter was badly shot up on the 26th, however, when Molnár claimed his 21st kill over Austria. Despite the battle damage, the ace successfully set his *Gustav* down at Szombathely airfield. Note that the fighter's tail marking lacks its white stripe.

## 16

**Bf 109G-6 V.8+53 of Lt Mihály Karátsonyi, 101/3 'Puma' FS, Veszprém, Hungary, Summer 1944**

One of the new breed of Hungarian fighter pilots, Karátsonyi scored five victories against the Americans in just a matter of weeks whilst defending Hungary in mid 1944. He was shot down in combat and severely burned on 7 August 1944, but was back in action by December. Karátsonyi was awarded the Iron Cross First and Second Class.

## 17

**Bf 109G-6/U2 W-0+20 of Sgt Mátyás Lörincz, 101/2 'Puma' FS, Veszprém, Hungary, Summer 1944**

Yet another novice when he was thrown into combat in the summer of 1944, then Cpl/Maj Lörincz scored two P-38 kills (and was indirectly responsible for the loss of a third Lightning) on his first mission on 16 June 1944. This unique feat earned him a field promotion to the rank of sergeant. Lörincz had increased his score to five when he was killed in action on 5 November 1944.

## 18

**Bf 109G-6/U2 (Wk-Nr 760381) W-0+21 of Lt László Dániel, 101/3 'Puma' FS, Veszprém, Hungary, Summer 1944**

The aircraft sported Dániel's white victory markers on its fin, a practice that was commonplace in the Luftwaffe but exceedingly rare in the Royal Hungarian Air Force. Dániel shared in the destruction of two B-24s and a P-38, claimed a second P-38 destroyed by himself and had a fourth Lightning declared unconfirmed destroyed, all during the course of 19 combat missions in June and July 1944.

## 19

**Bf 109G-6/U2 W-0+49 of Lt Kálmán Nánási, 101/3 'Puma' FS, Veszprém, Hungary, Summer 1944**

Nánási flew his first combat mission on 27 June 1944, and although he achieved no victories against the USAAF, he destroyed nine Soviet aircraft between December 1944 and March 1945.

## 20

**Bf 109G-6/U2 W-0+70 of 1/Lt Pál Irányi, First Officer of 101/I 'Puma' FG, Veszprém, Hungary, Summer 1944**

Irányi's G-6 is marked in the standard scheme worn by virtually all 101 FG machines in the late summer of 1944.

## 21

### Bf 109G-6 'Blue 4' of 1/Lt László Pottyondy, Commanding Officer of 102/2 'Ricsi' FS , Munkács, Hungary (now Mukachevo, in the Ukraine), October 1944

Two Hungarian fighter squadrons were in action on the Eastern Front during the autumn of 1944, with 13-kill ace Lászlo Pottyondy commanding 102/2 FS. Despite being constantly outnumbered, and struggling with a chronic shortage of aircraft, the veteran aces claimed half a dozen kills in the final months of 1944. This particular machine boasts the unit's rarely seen dog emblem on its cowling.

## 22

### Bf 109G-6 'Blue 14' of Capt László Pottyondy, Commanding Officer of 102/2 'Ricsi' FS, Budaörs, Hungary, November 1944

Promoted to captain in late October, Pottyondy regularly led his squadron on combined missions with III./JG 52, which shared the unit's new base at Budaörs. Lacking aircraft, 102/2 FS was finally integrated into 101 FG as its eighth squadron in December 1944.

## 23

### Bf 109G-6/U2 W-1+54 of Lt Kálmán Nánási, 101/5 'Puma' FS, early 1945

Nánási enjoyed considerable success with this machine in January 1945, destroying four Il-2s and a Yak-9 during the course of the month. His 39-mission career came to an end on 4 April 1945, when he was shot down and killed by Soviet flak during a ground-attack sortie.

## 24

### Bf 109G-6/U2 W-1+77 of Ens Dezső Szentgyörgyi, 101/2 'Puma' FS, Veszprém, Hungary, January 1945

Like Nánási, ranking Hungarian ace Szentgyörgyi did his best to stem the Soviet onslaught in January 1945 by downing three La-5s, two Yak-9s and an Il-2. Some of these kills were almost certainly claimed in this particular *Gustav*, which was written off late in the month by Cpl Varjas when he crashed attempting to take off in windy conditions. After Rumania switched to the Allied side on 28 September 1944, a yellow 'V' was painted on the underside of the left wing on all aircraft assigned to *Jafü Ost* to help flak crews distinguish friendly Bf 109s from Rumanian ones. The white segment of the Hungarian national marking was often left off, or overpainted with grey. The 'Puma' squadron emblem was routinely left off as well, due primarily to the groundcrews being kept busy keeping the *Gustavs* airworthy.

## 25

### Bf 109G-10 W-1+78 of Cpl/Maj Lajos Krascsenics, 101/3 'Puma' FS, Veszprém, Hungary, early 1945

Krascsenics' kills were all scored between November 1944 and January 1945, during which time he flew more than 40 missions.

## 26

### Bf 109G-10 W-1+83 of Lt László Dániel, 101/3 'Puma' FS, Veszprém, Hungary, early 1945

By this time Hungarian fighter pilots were flying combat missions almost exclusively against the Soviet Air Force.

Dániel enjoyed some success against his communist foes, despite being outnumbered every time he ventured aloft. Indeed, he claimed five kills in March 1945 alone. By war's end Dániel had completed 65 combat missions, and scored 8.5 kills.

## 27

### Bf 109G-6/U2 W-1+44 of Lt György Michna, 101/1 'Puma' FS, Veszprém, Hungary, February 1945

Another late war ace, Michna flew more than 30 combat missions and was credited with six victories. Two of these kills (Yak-9s) were claimed in this machine on 12 February 1945. By the end of the war Michna had been awarded the Iron Cross, First and Second Class.

## 28

### Bf 109G-6/U2 W-1+74 of Sgt/Maj István Fábián, 101/2 'Puma' FS, Veszprém, Hungary, February 1945

A veteran of nearly 100 combat missions, Fábián also cut a swathe through Soviet ranks in the final months of the conflict, claiming eight victories between November 1944 and March 1945. Two of these kills (La-5s) came on 19 February, almost certainly whilst Fábián was at the controls of this machine. One of the war's best wingmen, he was also one of the first Hungarian pilots to receive the Iron Cross First Class.

## 29

### Bf 109G-6/U2 W-1+71 of Lt József Málik, 101/2 'Puma' FS, Veszprém, Hungary, 9 March 1945

Málik, who was one of the youngest members of the unit, used this machine to down a Boston (taking his tally to 9.5 kills) on 9 March 1945 south-east of the besieged Hungarian airfield at Várpalota. Claiming his final victory (a Yak-9) exactly one week later, Málik lost his life on the ground during a low-level strafing attack by USAAF P-51s on Raffelding airfield, in Austria, on 16 April 1945.

## 30

### Bf 109G-10/U4 (Wk-Nr 613107) 'Yellow 5' of Ens István Fábián, 101/2 'Puma' FS , Veszprém, Hungary, March 1945

Fábián was promoted to the rank of ensign, in the field, on 12 March 1945. The following day he shot down an Il-2 south-west of Pázmánd, in Hungary, while flying this machine.

## 31

### Bf 109G-10/U4 (Wk-Nr 612778) 'Yellow 11' of Ens István Fábián, 101/2 'Puma' FS, Raffelding, Austria, 10 April 1945

Raffelding was the airfield from which the Hungarians flew their final combat missions of the war. 'Yellow 11', along with many other Hungarian aircraft, was destroyed on the ground in the strafing attack of 16 April 1945.

## 32

### Bf 109G-10/U4 'Yellow 10' of Cpl/Maj Ernö Kiss, 101/III 'Puma' FG, Raffelding, Austria, April 1945

Kiss scored five kills on the Eastern Front while with 102/1 FS in 1943-44, receiving the Iron Cross Second Class for his efforts. On 17 April 1945 he had the distinction of claiming the last aerial victory credited to a Hungarian in World War 2, almost certainly whilst flying this late-build *Gustav*.

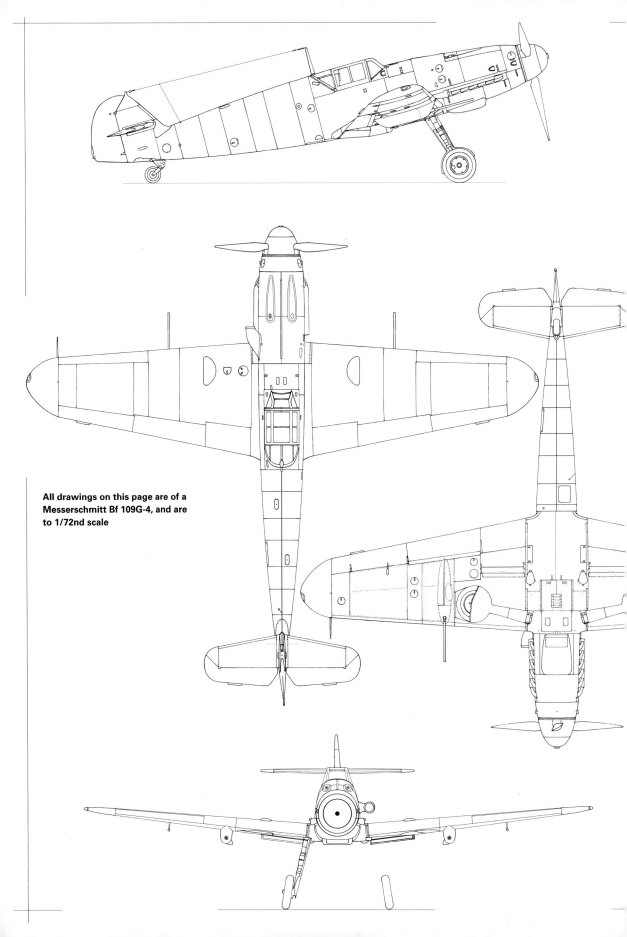

All drawings on this page are of a
Messerschmitt Bf 109G-4, and are
to 1/72nd scale

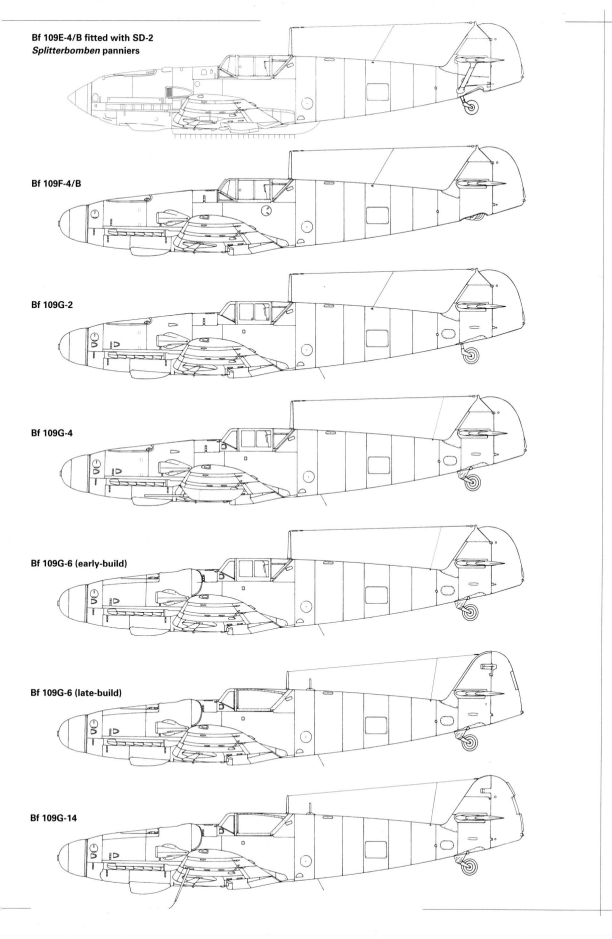

**Bf 109E-4/B fitted with SD-2**
*Splitterbomben* panniers

**Bf 109F-4/B**

**Bf 109G-2**

**Bf 109G-4**

**Bf 109G-6 (early-build)**

**Bf 109G-6 (late-build)**

**Bf 109G-14**

# INDEX

Figures in **bold** refer to illustrations

# FIND OUT MORE ABOUT OSPREY

❏ Please send me the latest listing of Osprey's publications

❏ I would like to subscribe to Osprey's e-mail newsletter

Title/rank _____

Name _____

Address _____

_____

_____

Postcode/zip _____ state/country _____

e-mail _____

I am interested in:

❏ Ancient world
❏ Medieval world
❏ 16th century
❏ 17th century
❏ 18th century
❏ Napoleonic
❏ 19th century

❏ American Civil War
❏ World War I
❏ World War II
❏ Modern warfare
❏ Military aviation
❏ Naval warfare

Please send to:

**USA & Canada**:
Osprey Direct USA, c/o MBI Publishing, P.O. Box 1,
729 Prospect Avenue, Osceola, WI 54020

**UK, Europe and rest of world**:
Osprey Direct UK, P.O. Box 140, Wellingborough,
Northants, NN8 2FA, United Kingdom

OSPREY
PUBLISHING

www.ospreypublishing.com

call our telephone hotline
for a free information pack

USA & Canada: 1-800-826-6600
UK, Europe and rest of world call:
+44 (0) 1933 443 863

**P-51D**
**of Lt Col Glenn T Eagleston,**
**353rd Fighter Squadron**
Profile taken from *Aviation Elite 7:*
*354th Fighter Group*
Published by Osprey
Profiles by Chris Davey
& John Weal

**Tomahawk**
Illustration taken from *Aircraft of the Aces 38:*
*Tomahawk and Kittyhawk Aces of the RAF and Commonwealth*
Published by Osprey
Illustrated by Iain Wyllie

POSTCARD

www.ospreypublishing.com